Sareena A. ♥mom

Cooking Light®
way to
cook
vegetarian

ISBN-13: 978-0-8487-3992-8
ISBN-10: 0-8487-3992-2
Library of Congress Control Number: 2013934192
Printed in the United States of America
Third printing 2013

Be sure to check with your health-care provider before making any changes in your diet.

Oxmoor House

VP, Publishing Director: Jim Childs
Brand Manager: Michelle Turner Aycock
Editorial Director: Susan Payne Dobbs
Senior Editor: Heather Averett
Managing Editor: Laurie S. Herr

Cooking Light. Way to Cook Vegetarian

Editor: Rachel Quinlivan, R.D.
Project Editor: Vanessa Lynn Rusch
Senior Designer: Emily Albright Parrish
Test Kitchens Director: Elizabeth Tyler Austin
Assistant Director,
Test Kitchens: Julie Christopher
Test Kitchens Professionals: Allison E. Cox, Julie Gunter, Kathleen Royal Phillips, Catherine Crowell Steele, Ashley T. Strickland
Photography Director: Jim Bathie
Senior Photo Stylist: Kay E. Clarke
Associate Photo Stylist: Katherine Eckert Coyne
Senior Production Manager: Greg A. Amason

Contributors

Compositor: Teresa Cole
Copy Editor: Norma Butterworth-McKittrick
Indexer: Mary Ann Laurens
Interns: Ina Ables, Sarah Bélanger, Torie Cox, Georgia Dodge, Perri K. Hubbard, Maggie McDaris, Allison Sperando, Caitlin Watzke

Cooking Light.

Editor: Scott Mowbray
Creative Director: Carla Frank
Deputy Editor: Phillip Rhodes
Food Editor: Ann Taylor Pittman
Special Publications Editor: Mary Simpson Creel, M.S., R.
Nutrition Editor: Kathy Kitchens Downie, R.D.
Associate Food Editors: Timothy Q. Cebula, Julianna Grimes
Associate Editors: Cindy Hatcher, Brandy Rushing
Test Kitchens Director: Vanessa T. Pruett
Assistant Test Kitchens Director: Tiffany Vickers Davis
Chief Food Stylist: Charlotte Fekete
Senior Food Stylist: Kellie Gerber Kelley
Recipe Testers and Developers: Robin Bashinsky, Deb Wise
Art Director: Fernande Bondarenko
Junior Deputy Art Director: Alexander Spacher
Designer: Chase Turberville
Photo Director: Kristen Schaefer
Senior Photographer: Randy Mayor
Senior Photo Stylist: Cindy Barr
Photo Stylist: Leigh Ann Ross
Copy Chief: Maria Parker Hopkins
Assistant Copy Chief: Susan Roberts
Research Editor: Michelle Gibson Daniels
Editorial Production Director: Liz Rhoades
Production Editor: Hazel R. Eddins
Art/Production Assistant: Josh Rutledge
Administrative Coordinator: Carol D. Johnson
Cookinglight.com Editor: Allison Long Lowery
Production Assistant: Mallory Daugherty

To order additional publications, call 1-800-765-6400 or 1-800-491-0551.

For more books to enrich your life, visit **oxmoorhouse.com**

To search, savor, and share thousands of recipes, visit **myrecipes.com**

Cooking Light®

way to cook vegetarian

Oxmoor
House®

Contents

Welcome

More and more Americans are falling in love with vegetarian cooking. Some are experimenting with the Meatless Monday idea—enjoying one or more vegetarian days per week as they explore healthier cooking.

Others are simply choosing to incorporate more vegetarian meals into their diet when they return from farmers' markets laden with produce so good it requires no bacon or beef to satisfy. Others have set off down a completely vegetarian path for health or ethical reasons. This book will help any cook who is exploring the vegetarian option.

Vegetarian eating has been around for ages, but lately in the West it has shed its reputation of being nutritionally complicated. No longer do we worry about getting enough protein—there's plenty in beans, nuts, eggs (if you eat them), grains, and soy, all eaten in balance. Smothering dishes with cheese and butter to compensate for lack of meat is also completely passé.

Yet it's hard to overstate the nutritional appeal of plants. No foods are really "superfoods," but grains, fruits, and vegetables burst with a huge variety of vitamins, minerals, antioxidants, healthy fats, and fiber that come together to form the best possible diet. Technique is important, of course, whether you're working with unfamiliar vegetables or grains (fava beans or quinoa), or with delicious soy foods such as tempeh or tofu.

Today's vegetarian cooking celebrates the amazing, delicious natural bounty of the earth: the crunchy, intense joys of fruits and vegetables in peak conditions along with the chewy pleasures of whole grains mixed with herbs and spices. And it draws from so many of the great cuisines of the world: Indian, Chinese, Mexican, and Arabic, as well as the superb vegetable cookery of France, Italy, and America.

It's with new satisfaction, then, that you can contemplate the old entreaty from your childhood dinner table: *eat your vegetables!*

Scott Mowbray,
Editor

the CookingLight® way to cook
vegetarian

vegetarian

This book is filled with vegetarian recipes and techniques to help you prepare and savor meat-free meals. Vegetarian diets can certainly meet all your nutritional needs—the key is to eat a variety of foods so all your nutrient bases are covered. Here we share our healthy eating principles for a well-rounded vegetarian diet.

healthy eating principle 1 Think about protein

You can easily meet your daily protein needs by eating an array of plant-based foods. Fill out your meals with beans, lentils, nuts, rice, and soy products like tofu and tempeh. Don't rely on a hefty portion of cheese to fill the protein gap since cheeses often add saturated fat.

healthy eating principle 2 Consider calcium

The mineral calcium plays a vital role in overall health, including achieving and maintaining healthy teeth and bones. Vegetarians can meet their calcium requirement by including calcium-rich dairy products (milk, cheese, and yogurt) in meals and snacks. (One 8-ounce glass o

ilk provides 256 milligrams of calcium, which is about
ne-fourth of the recommended daily intake of 1,000
illigrams per day for adults age 50 and under and
200 milligrams for age 51 and older recommended by
e Institute of Medicine.)

   If you're lactose intolerant, a vegan, or simply want
 incorporate other nondairy sources of calcium into
our diet, you have options. Some of those other
ources include fortified breakfast cereals, soy products
uch as tofu made with calcium sulfate and soy milk,
oybeans, soynuts, calcium-fortified fruit juices, and
ome dark-green leafy vegetables including collard
eens, turnip greens, mustard greens, bok choy,
roccoli, Chinese cabbage, kale, and okra. When you
e shopping for tofu, be sure to look carefully at the
utrition label to verify that the tofu you are buying is
ade with calcium sulfate; nigari (magnesium chloride)
 another common coagulating agent used to make
fu, but it has a lower calcium content.

   Keep in mind that calcium can be finicky. According
 the U.S. Department of Agriculture (USDA), the
alcium absorption from most foods, including dairy
roducts and grains, is about the same, but calcium
an be poorly absorbed from foods high in oxalic acid

(found in spinach, sweet potatoes, and beans) or phytic
acid (found in unleavened bread, raw beans, seeds, and
nuts). These acids bind with the calcium in these foods
and prevent its absorption, but they don't prevent the
absorption of calcium from other foods eaten at the
same time. It's best to eat a variety of calcium-rich
foods over the course of the day to make sure you
are meeting your needs.

When it comes to fruits and vegetables, more matters (and color counts)

Whole fruits and vegetables are some of the best foods you can eat. They are low in calories, high in fiber, and brimming with vitamins, minerals, and antioxidants. They play an important role in staving off heart disease and stroke, managing blood pressure and cholesterol, helping prevent certain types of cancer, protecting vision, and maintaining a healthy digestive system.

And color is certainly key—the vitamins and phytochemicals that give plants their brilliant colors work as antioxidants, immune boosters, and anti-inflammatories in humans.

The best way to benefit from these healthy compounds is to eat a variety of fresh produce based on color; you can use the tools at MyPyramid.gov to figure out how many fruits and vegetables you need to eat each day.

Eat seasonally

nce fruits and vegetables are an important part of a getarian diet, flavor and freshness are vital, and the st way to achieve both is to buy fruits and vegetables season. This practice offers a variety of benefits. When you buy fresh produce in season, you don't ve to do much to them to make them taste extraordi- ry. From the arrival of summer's squashes, peaches, d tomatoes to the cranberries, oranges, and Brussels routs you'll find in winter, each season offers some-

thing unique and delicious to keep your palate happy.

Eating fruits and vegetables at the peak of fresh- ness is also a boon to your health as well as your wallet. You'll benefit from all the vitamins, minerals, fiber, and antioxidants these colorful plants have to offer, and since there's often an abundance of fruits and vegeta- bles during the harvest season, you're more apt to find bargains at the grocery store. For more information, see our Seasonal Produce Guide on page 409.

healthy
eating
principle

Go for whole grains

All grains start out as whole grains, which means that they still contain the germ, endosperm, and bran. The bran is full of filling fiber, which keeps you full, while the germ and endosperm contain beneficial antioxidants, vitamins, minerals, and other healthful compounds. Processing, however, can remove one or more of these components, making refined grains less healthful. Research has shown that eating whole grains helps lower your risk for heart disease, obesity, diabetes, high blood pressure, and high cholesterol. For more information about whole grains, see page 70.

Also remember iron, zinc, and B$_{12}$

In addition to protein and calcium, vegetarians need to get adequate amounts of iron, zinc, and vitamin B$_{12}$. Iron carries oxygen in the blood, and iron deficiency can leave you feeling tired. Vegetarian sources of iron include iron-fortified cereals as well as spinach, kidney beans, black-eyed peas, lentils, turnip greens, whole-wheat breads, peas, dried apricots, prunes, and raisins.

Zinc is necessary for a variety of functions including helping maintain the immune system and keeping it functioning properly. Zinc sources include a variety of beans (white beans, kidney beans, and chickpeas), cereals fortified with zinc, wheat germ, milk and milk products, and pumpkinseeds.

Vitamin B$_{12}$ is found primarily in animal products and some fortified foods. Vegetarians can get it from milk products, eggs, and B$_{12}$-fortified products including some breakfast cereals, soy-based beverages, and vegetable burgers.

And don't forget fiber

Not only are high-fiber foods tasty (think hearty stews with beans and desserts with fresh apples and pears), but they also help control hunger, lower cholesterol, and maintain digestive health. Fiber is the part of plant foods that our body can't digest or absorb into the bloodstream, which means it doesn't provide us with any calories, but it does flush the digestive system as it moves through our bodies.

The Academy of Nutrition and Dietetics recommends eating 20 to 35 grams of fiber daily, but estimates show that most of us fall short of that, consuming only about 14 grams daily. Boosting your fiber intake is easier than you might think. It helps to think in groups of 10—getting 10 grams in the morning, 10 at lunch, and 10 at dinner. Swap your standard breads and pastas for 100-percent whole-wheat varieties. Trade out your

breakfast cereals for bran or oatmeal, and whole-wheat couscous for white rice—little changes like these add up to big benefits. Here are some other simple substitutions and tips:

• **Eat the skin.** Whether it's an apple, pear, or potato, most of the fiber is in the skin.

• **Read the Nutrition Facts** labels for cereals. While 5 grams of fiber is good, 8 grams or more is better.

• **Choose breads and crackers** that have at least 2 grams of fiber per slice or serving.

• **Cook vegetables briefly.** The longer vegetables cook, the more fiber they lose. Try steaming them until they're crisp-tender to retain most of the fiber content. Also snack on raw vegetables. Salads, with their vegetables and seeds or nuts toppings, make a good high-fiber option.

breakfast   snack

lunch   dinner sides

Meeting Your Daily Fiber Needs

Breakfast
5 grams: 1¼ cups bite-sized whole-wheat cereal biscuits (such as bite-sized Shredded Wheat)
1 gram: 2 tablespoon raisins
4 grams: 1 medium banana

Lunch
2 grams: 2 cups mixed greens salad
2 grams: ¼ cup cooked artichoke hearts
2 grams: 3 tablespoons chickpeas (garbanzo beans)
1 gram: 1 tablespoon slivered almonds

Snack
4 grams: 1 medium pear

Dinner sides
5 grams: 1 cup steamed broccoli
5 grams: 1 (4-ounce) baked sweet potato with skin

Total: 31 grams

Vegans

Cooking Light Way to Cook Vegetarian, we've
focused on a broad interpretation of a vegetarian diet,
which includes eggs and dairy products. For those who
follow a vegan diet, which means no animal products
of any kind including eggs, milk, cheese, yogurt, and
other dairy products, we've identified recipes that meet
those criteria with each recipe and in the recipe index,
which starts on page 418. Again, we've focused on the
widest interpretation of a vegan diet, so some of the
recipes we've identified as vegan do include honey.

way to cook vegetarian

appetizers

appetizers

Appetizers can be the perfect way to begin a meal, or they can be the perfect small meal. Little bites can stave off hunger, allowing you to linger longer, or they can provide a light meal when heavier foods aren't appetizing. Regardless of how you choose to enjoy appetizers, vegetarian options shine.

Vegetarian Appetizers

Vegetable trays and cheese and crackers are common vegetarian staples on party tables, but meatless appetizers don't have to be so boring. These small bites can be the perfect way to showcase the extraordinary flavor of fresh vegetables mixed with an array of spices or enjoy a variety of plant-based dips and spreads. This chapter brings you a sampling of recipes that are anything but ordinary.

A Global Custom

Appetizers and small plates of food are an international custom. You can find them served all around the Mediterranean. In Spain, they're called tapas. In France, they're called hors d'oeuvres; in Italy, antipasti. In Greece, Turkey, Syria, Lebanon, Israel, and Egypt, they use the word meze; and in Morocco, *mukbalatt*. Even Venice has its own custom of *cicheti,* the local equivalent of tapas and meze. In every Mediterranean country, people love to meet with friends after work for a drink and a bite to eat.

ow to Create a
reat Cheese Plate

eparing a cheese course can
 as simple or as elaborate as you
. A selection of cheeses makes
delicious and sophisticated first
urse or dessert.

To choose three to five varieties—
 number recommended for a
eese course selection—consider

creating a theme. Focus on a country, region, or province. For example,
choose types of cow's milk cheese
from the Normandy region of
France, or varieties of goat cheese
from the Poitou-Charentes region
of western France. Another option
is to select by texture and type. A
blue cheese platter might include
Gorgonzola, Roquefort, and Stilton;

if you'd like a semisoft offering, try
Havarti, fontina, and mozzarella.

Whichever you serve, always
provide a separate knife for each
cheese so the flavors do not
intermingle. Use a wide, blunt
knife for softer cheeses so they'll
be easier to spread. Harder
cheeses will need a sharp knife
to make a clean cut.

dips

kitchen how-to: roast garlic

When garlic is roasted, its flavor mellows to nutty and slightly sweet, and it softens into a spread that has the consistency of butter.

1. Remove the white papery skin from the garlic head (do not peel or separate the cloves). Cut off the top third of the head; discard.

2. Drizzle 1 teaspoon oil over the cut side of the garlic; wrap the garlic in foil. Bake it until tender.

3. Separate the cloves, and squeeze them to extract the garlic pulp. Discard the skins.

bruschetta

Bruschetta is simple to make. It starts with a baguette or narrow loaf that has been thinly sliced and toasted. To that crunchy bread base, add any toppings you wish—a mixture of vegetables drizzle with olive oil and fresh herbs or a flavorful cheese mixture spread on and topped with chopped olives. Feel free to experiment on your own. The options are endless.

{vegan recipe}
Spicy Stir-Fried Mushroom Bruschetta

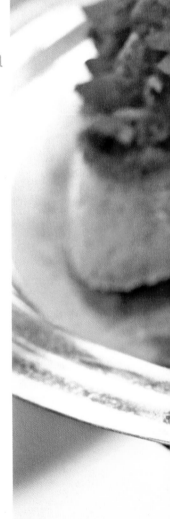

- 1 tablespoon canola oil
- ½ teaspoon cumin seeds
- 1 whole dried red chile
- 1½ teaspoons grated peeled fresh ginger
- 1 cup finely chopped red onion
- 2 tablespoons dried fenugreek leaves (kasoori methi)
- ¼ teaspoon salt
- 1 minced seeded jalapeño pepper
- 1½ teaspoons ground coriander
- ⅛ teaspoon ground red pepper
- 2 garlic cloves, minced
- 2 cups quartered mushrooms
- 1 cup (½-inch) cubed tomato
- 7 tablespoons no-salt-added tomato sauce
- 3 tablespoons chopped fresh cilantro, divided
- ⅛ teaspoon garam masala
- 8 (1-ounce) slices country bread, toasted

1. Heat first 3 ingredients in a large skillet over medium-high heat; sauté 1 minute or until cumin begins to darken. Add ginger to pan; sauté 30 seconds. Add red onion and fenugreek; sauté 2 minutes or until onion is tender. Add salt and jalapeño; saute 2 minutes or until onion softens and begins to brown. Add coriander, red pepper, and minced garlic; sauté 30 seconds. Add mushrooms; cook 7 minutes or until liquid evaporates. Stir in tomato, tomato sauce, 2 tablespoons cilantro, and garam masala; bring to a simmer. Cook 15 minutes or until sauce thickens. Sprinkle with remaining 1 tablespoon cilantro. Serve with bread. **Yield: 8 servings (serving size: 3½ tablespoons mushroom mixture and 1 bread slice).**

CALORIES 110; FAT 2.2g (sat 0.2g, mono 1.1g, poly 0.7g); PROTEIN 4.2g; CARB 19.1g; FIBER 1.9g; CHOL 0mg; IRON 1.8mg; SODIUM 238mg; CALC 23mg

Garam Masala
What it adds: This mixture of ground spices can vary from region to region in India, but all add an intense variety of flavors.

Fenugreek
What it adds: A component of some curry powders, fenugreek adds an earthy, subtly bitter essence to Indian dishes. Omit if you can't find it.

Dried Chiles
What they add: Along with the ground red pepper, the dried chiles deliver spicy heat.

vegetable appetizers

Vegetables are the perfect appetizer food. They can be cut into bite-sized pieces and filled, topped, and coated with a variety of delicious accompaniments.

tchen how-to:
nake windowpane potato chips

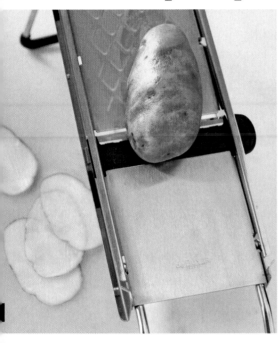

mandoline will help you create picture-perfect chips.
: Buy an extra potato to practice with beforehand.

Adjust the mandoline to the thinnest setting, and cut
ch potato lengthwise into paper-thin slices. You'll need
discard the first few smaller slices of each potato.
Arrange half of the potato slices on a baking sheet.
p each slice with an herb sprig that fits into the center.
p each piece with another potato slice of
 same size, and press gently to adhere. Cover the
tato stacks with parchment paper.
To ensure that the potato slices seal around the herbs
d cook into a flat disk, place another baking sheet
 top of the slices, and top with a cast-iron or other
avy skillet.

dumplings

As a general rule, prepared dumpling dough shouldn't stand too long. Cook dumplings soon after they're formed and eat them soon after they're cooked. Little pockets of steam trapped inside make them tender; once the steam dissipates, the dumplings toughen and become dense.

damame Dumplings

k for round gyoza wrappers in the refrigerated
duce section of the grocery store. Wonton
appers are lightly coated with cornstarch, which
kes them easier to work with.

ce:
- tablespoons chopped green onions
- tablespoons less-sodium soy sauce
- teaspoon honey

mplings:
- cup frozen shelled edamame (green soybeans)
- teaspoon fresh lemon juice
- teaspoon dark sesame oil
- teaspoon ground cumin
- teaspoon salt
- wonton wrappers
- teaspoons cornstarch
- poking spray
- cup water, divided

o prepare sauce, combine first 3 ingredients in a
all bowl, stirring with a whisk.

2. To prepare dumplings, cook edamame according to package directions; drain. Rinse edamame with cold water; drain well. Combine edamame and next 4 ingredients in a food processor; process until smooth.
3. Working with 1 wonton wrapper at a time (cover remaining wrappers with a damp towel to prevent drying), spoon about 1 teaspoon edamame mixture onto center of each wrapper; Moisten edges of dough with water; fold opposite corners to form a triangle, pinching points to seal. Place dumplings on a large baking sheet sprinkled with cornstarch.
4. Heat a large nonstick skillet over medium-high heat; coat pan with cooking spray. Arrange half of dumplings in a single layer in pan, and reduce heat to medium. Cook 1 minute or until bottoms begin to brown; turn. Add ¼ cup water to pan; cover. Cook 30 seconds; uncover. Cook 1 minute or until liquid evaporates. Repeat procedure with remaining dumplings and water. Serve immediately with sauce. **Yield: 10 servings (serving size: 2 dumplings and about 1 teaspoon sauce).**

CALORIES 71; FAT 1.3g (sat 0.1g, mono 0.2g, poly 0.3g); PROTEIN 3g; CARB 11.7g; FIBER 1g; CHOL 1mg; IRON 0.8mg; SODIUM 272mg; CALC 17mg

tchen how-to: make edamame dumplings

For these dumplings, scoop 1 scant teaspoon of the edamame mixture onto the center of each wrapper. While it may seem small, it's the perfect amount for these dumplings.

grape leaves

Grape leaves are a part of Turkish, Greek, Arab, and Romanian cuisines and are often stuffed with a mixture of rice, vegetables, meat, and spices. They're served warm or cold as an appetizer or main dish with yogurt.

egan recipe }
rape Leaves Stuffed with
ice, Currants, and Herbs

- large grape leaves
- ooking spray
- cup finely chopped onion
- cup uncooked long-grain rice
- cup chopped green onions
- tablespoons pine nuts
- cup water
- tablespoons dried currants
- tablespoons chopped fresh flat-leaf parsley
- tablespoons chopped fresh mint
- tablespoons chopped fresh dill
- teaspoon salt
- teaspoon freshly ground black pepper
- teaspoon ground cinnamon
- cup plain fat-free yogurt
- lemon wedges

Rinse grape leaves with cold water; drain well. Pat dry
h paper towels. Remove stems; discard. Set aside.
Heat a large nonstick skillet over medium heat; coat
n with cooking spray. Add 1 cup chopped onion; cook
inutes or until tender, stirring occasionally. Add rice,
en onions, and nuts; cook 4 minutes, stirring frequent-
Stir in water and next 7 ingredients; bring to a boil.
ver, reduce heat, and simmer 15 minutes or until rice is
der. Cool slightly.
Spoon 1 rounded tablespoon rice mixture onto center
each grape leaf. Fold one side of leaf over filling. Fold
oosite side of leaf over filling. Beginning at 1 short side,
up leaf tightly, jelly-roll fashion. Steam grape leaves,
vered, 10 minutes or until thoroughly heated. Cool to
m temperature. Serve with yogurt and lemon wedges.
ld: 8 servings (serving size: 3 stuffed grape
ves, 1 tablespoon yogurt, and 1 lemon wedge).

ORIES 88; FAT 1.8g (sat 0.2g, mono 0.4g, poly 0.9g); PROTEIN 2.7g; CARB 16.5g;
R 1g; CHOL 0mg; IRON 1.3mg; SODIUM 500mg; CALC 72mg

kitchen how-to:
assemble stuffed grape leaves

Before assembling stuffed grape leaves,
rinse the leaves with cold water, and drain them
well. Pat them dry with paper towels, and then
remove and discard the stems.

1. Spoon 1 tablespoon of the filling mixture onto
the center of each grape leaf.
2. Fold one side of the leaf over the filling.
3. Fold the opposite side of the leaf over the filling.
4. Beginning at the short side, roll up the leaf
tightly, jelly-roll fashion.

way to cook vegetarian

breads

breads

Since most breads are vegetarian by nature, they naturally fit into a meatless diet. Here we've provided a sampling of healthy recipe to round out your meals or use as snacks or meals on their own. Light baking starts with the same ingredients as traditional baking—flour, salt, sugar, butter, and eggs. The difference is in the proportions of the ingredients and the additions that yield healthy but still delicious results.

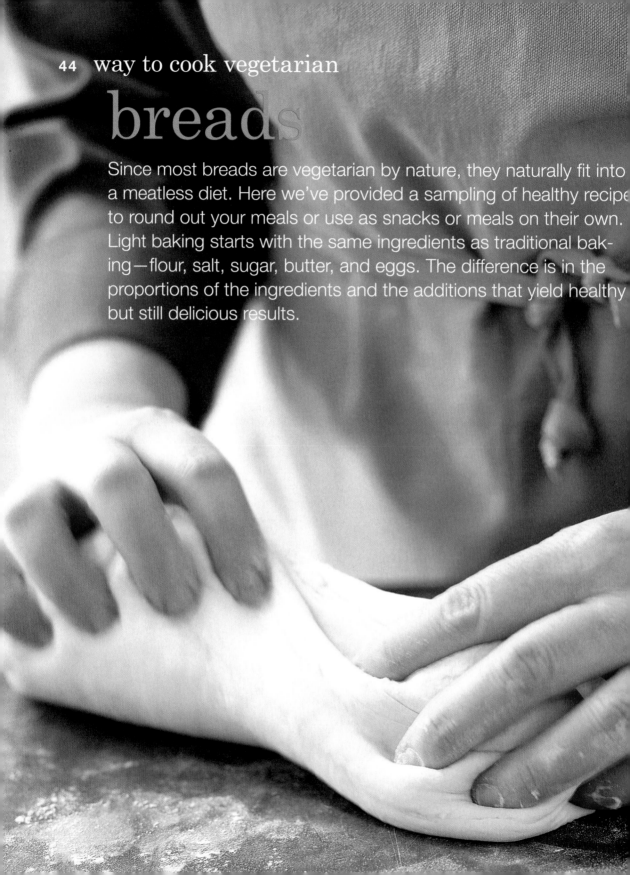

e Importance of Fat and Sugar

in the form of butter and shortening, and sugar
play a crucial role in baked products. Butter
es the flavor of other ingredients, creates a fine
ure, and helps make baked goods tender by coating
flour proteins and preventing them from forming
en (gluten makes dough strong, but it can also make
ugh). Don't substitute light or whipped butter or
garine for butter; these products have added
er and air, which can alter the texture.

e)heating It Up

aking, temperature control is vital. To get the best
lts and maximum volume, preheat your oven to the
cified temperature. You'll need to do the same for

quick breads prepared on your griddle, in a waffle iron,
or on a nonstick skillet. You can check the griddle by
sprinkling a few drops of water on the surface. The
temperature is correct when the water dances on the
surface of the pan and evaporates within a few seconds.
It's too hot if the water bubbles and immediately
evaporates. It's not hot enough if it takes several
seconds for the water to appear to boil.

Do Not Divide (or Multiply) and Conquer

You shouldn't halve, double, or otherwise multiply
or divide a recipe because the ratio of wet to dry
ingredients can change as volumes of both increase
or decrease. The result can be undesirable.

tchen how-to: measure flour

**important to use the type of flour specified
the recipe** because different flours have varying
els of proteins that, when combined with liquid, form
ten, a stretchy substance that makes breads elastic
d strong.

Although using the right flour is key, once you've got
right flour or a suitable substitute (see the substitution
de on page 406), the second most important factor is
per measuring. Precision is crucial in light baking

since too much flour can create a dry product. To
prevent this, it's best to measure by weight. You'll need a
kitchen scale to get an accurate weight. If you don't have
one, you can still use your measuring cups. Here's how:

1. Lightly spoon the flour into dry measuring cups
without compacting it.
2. Level off the excess flour with the flat edge of a
knife.

kitchen how-to: make yeast bread

1

2

Anyone can make yeast bread—it just takes a little patience and clear instruction. To get started, all you need are measuring cups and spoons, a large glass bowl, a wooden spoon, a flat surface on which to knead the bread, an oven, and a wire cooling rack. Glass bowls and wooden spoons are preferable to metal, which can react with the dough and affect the bread's flavor.

Before getting started, be sure to check the expiration date on the yeast, buy the type of flour specified in the recipe, and use bottled water if your local tap water has any unpleasant smells or flavors.

1. In the first step, the dry yeast is dissolved (or proofed) in water warmed to 100° to 110°. First-timers take note: It's always a good idea to use a thermometer to measure the temperature of the water until you feel comfortable recognizing the target temperature. You can also test the warmth of the liquid on the inside of your wrist—it should feel no warmer than a hot shower. About 5 minutes after mixing the yeast with the warm water, the mixture will start to bubble. If it doesn't bubble, the water was either too hot, which killed the yeast, or too cold, which

inhibited its growth.

2. The remaining ingredients are added to the yeast mixture to cre a dough. Turn the dough out ontc smooth, lightly floured surface, ar lightly flour your hands. Using the heel of your hands, push the dou away from you.

3. Lift the edge farthest away fror you, and fold it toward you. Give dough a quarter turn. Repeat step 2 and 3 until the dough feels smo and elastic; this usually takes abc

kitchen how-to: make muffins

A well-made muffin has a rounded, even shape and a pebbly top, while an overmixed muffin will be peaked and have a coarse, tough texture.

1. Combine the dry ingredients, and make a well in the center of the mixture using the back of a spoon.
2. Combine the liquid ingredients, and pour them into the well. For well-rounded muffins, a lumpy batter is best. Stir the batter gently just until the dry ingredients are moistened; a smooth batter is not essential. Then spoon the batter into muffin cups coated with cooking spray or lined with liners that have been coated with cooking spray, and bake according to the recipe directions. After the muffins have finished baking, remove them from the pans as soon as possible to keep condensation from forming and making them soggy on the bottom.

all about dates

We often use soft and semidry dates, which are less sweet and more aromatic than fully dried fruit. Unless a recipe specifies a variety, any of the following will work.

Soft dates have the highest moisture content and should be stored in the refrigerator.
1. Medjool: These dates are dark brown, sweet, rich in flavor, meaty, moist, and sticky. In general, they are the largest type of date, but they vary greatly in size.
2. Amer Hajj: These dates are similar in color to Medjools, but they are spicier with a caramel flavor and have a soft, sticky texture. They are called "the visitor's date" in the Middle East, where they are a delicacy served to guests. Their shape is similar to plum tomatoes, but they are smaller.
3. Halaway: These light brown to blond dates have a sweet, buttery flavor and thick flesh.
4. Barhi: These dates have amber-colored skin. They're soft, not too sweet, and have a light, buttery, caramel flavor.

Semidry dates are firmer and should be stored in a dark, cool place.
5. Deglet Noor: Amber-colored, elongated Deglet Noor dates have a delicate honey flavor, are firmer than Amer Hajj, and are not as sweet or moist as Medjool. They're the most popular date sold in the United States; in grocery stores they are often in round packages labeled "fresh pitted dates."
6. Empress: These dates have a yellow crown at the top. They're soft, not too sweet, and a bit chewy with a deep caramel flavor.
7. Zahidi: A Zahidi date has a large seed and fibrous flesh. This variety is often diced for recipes. The flavor is similar to brown sugar.

Peanut Butter and Jelly Muffins

Consider these a breakfast version of a peanut butter and jelly sandwich. Don't use a natural-style peanut butter in this recipe; it won't have enough sugar or fat to help the muffins rise.

4.5 ounces all-purpose flour (about 1 cup)
3.5 ounces whole-wheat flour (about ¾ cup)
¼ cup granulated sugar
¼ cup packed dark brown sugar
1 tablespoon baking powder
½ teaspoon salt
1¼ cups fat-free milk
⅓ cup creamy peanut butter
¼ cup egg substitute
2 tablespoons butter, melted
1 teaspoon vanilla extract
Cooking spray
¼ cup strawberry jam

1. Preheat oven to 400°.
2. Weigh or lightly spoon flours into dry measuring cups; level with a knife. Combine flours, sugars, baking powder, and salt in a large bowl; stir with a whisk. Make a well in center of mixture. Combine milk and next 4 ingredients; add to flour mixture, stirring just until moist.
3. Spoon batter into 12 muffin cups coated with cooking spray. Fill each cup half full with batter. Spoon 1 teaspoon jam into each cup. Spoon remaining batter on top to cover jam. Bake at 400° for 20 minutes or until muffins spring back when touched lightly in center. Let cool in pan 5 minutes. Remove from pan, and cool on a wire rack. **Yield: 1 dozen (serving size: 1 muffin).**

CALORIES 185; FAT 5.8g (sat 2g, mono 2.3g, poly 1.2g); PROTEIN 5.2g; CARB 29.4g; FIBER 1.6g; CHOL 5.6mg; IRON 1.2mg; SODIUM 288mg; CALC 113mg

kitchen how-to:
make peanut butter and jelly muffins

Spoon the batter into 12 muffin cups coated with cooking spray, filling them half full. Spoon 1 teaspoon jam into each cup, and then spoon the remaining batter on top to cover the jam.

quick bread loaves

Many quick bread loaves benefit from the same gentle mixing technique used for muffins. Be sure to let the loaves cool completely before slicing them so they won't crumble. Use a sharp, serrated knife and a gentle sawing motion to cut them.

Banana-Cinnamon Waffles

Crown these lightly spiced waffles with cinnamon sugar, sliced bananas, and/or a drizzle of maple syrup. Buckwheat flour adds a somewhat tangy, robust nuttiness.

4.5 ounces all-purpose flour (about 1 cup)
2.4 ounces whole-wheat flour (about ½ cup)
 1 ounce buckwheat flour (about ¼ cup)
 ¼ cup ground flaxseed
 2 tablespoons sugar
1½ teaspoons baking powder
 ½ teaspoon ground cinnamon
 ¼ teaspoon salt
1½ cups fat-free milk
 3 tablespoons butter, melted
 2 large eggs, lightly beaten
 1 large ripe banana, mashed
 Cooking spray

1. Weigh or lightly spoon flours into dry measuring cups; level with a knife. Combine flours, flaxseed, and next 4 ingredients in a medium bowl, stirring with a whisk.
2. Combine milk, butter, and eggs, stirring with a whisk; add milk mixture to flour mixture, stirring until blended. Fold in mashed banana.
3. Preheat a waffle iron. Coat iron with cooking spray. Spoon about ¼ cup batter per 4-inch waffle onto hot waffle iron, spreading batter to edges. Cook 3 to 4 minutes or until steaming stops; repeat procedure with remaining batter. **Yield: 8 servings (serving size: 2 waffles).**

CALORIES 215; FAT 7.4g (sat 3.3g, mono 1.9g, poly 1.4g); PROTEIN 7.3g; CARB 31.1g; FIBER 3.4g; CHOL 65mg; IRON 1.9mg; SODIUM 205mg; CALC 133mg

breadsticks

Serve breadsticks alongside soups or salads. You can bake the breadsticks the night before, cool them to room temperature, and store them in an airtight container; serve them at room temperature, or reheat them in the microwave the next day.

kitchen how-to: make breadsticks

If you prefer, you can make the entire batch with just one of the toppings. For milder heat, substitute pickled banana peppers for the jalapeños, or experiment with your own topping combinations.

1. Unroll the dough, and cut it in half crosswise. Sprinkle 1 dough half with cheese and peppers (or any toppings you wish); press the toppings lightly into the dough. Cut the dough half in half crosswise.

2. Cut the dough into 12 strips. Twist each piece into a 6-inch-long strip; place on a baking sheet. Repeat process with the other dough half, topping it with Parmesan and olives (or any toppings you wish). Bake.

1   2

Breadsticks Two Ways

1 **(11-ounce) can refrigerated soft breadstick dough**
2 **tablespoons reduced-fat shredded cheddar cheese**
1 **tablespoon diced pickled jalapeño peppers**
2 **tablespoons grated fresh Parmesan cheese**
1 **tablespoon minced pitted kalamata olives**

1. Preheat oven to 375°.
2. Unroll dough; cut in half crosswise. Sprinkle 1 dough half with cheddar cheese and peppers; press lightly into dough. Cut dough half in half crosswise. Separate dough into 12 strips. Twist each piece into a 6-inch-long strip; place on a baking sheet.
3. Sprinkle Parmesan and olives over second half of dough; press lightly into dough. Cut dough half in half crosswise. Separate dough into 12 strips. Twist each piece into a 6-inch-long strip; place on a second baking sheet. Bake breadsticks at 375° for 12 minutes or until golden brown. Cool on wire racks. **Yield: 24 breadsticks (serving size: 2 breadsticks).**

CALORIES 83; FAT 2.1g (sat 0.7g, mono 0.6g, poly 0.5g); PROTEIN 2.6g; CARB 12.8g; FIBER 0.4g; CHOL 1mg; IRON 0.8mg; SODIUM 247mg; CALC 20mg

yeast breads

Even though it may seem intimidating, anyone can bake yeast breads. Just follow the steps carefully, and you'll be rewarded with beautiful breads to grace your table. See page 46 to learn more about the technique.

Walnut and Rosemary Loaves

The technique of these loaves is classic, with two rises, easy boule shaping, and a golden egg-wash glaze. Inside the dark crust is a creamy white bread flecked with rosemary and bits of walnuts. This bread is great with soups, excellent for sandwiches, and delicious toasted and spread with apple butter for breakfast.

> 2 cups warm 1% low-fat milk (100° to 110°)
> ¼ cup warm water (100° to 110°)
> 3 tablespoons sugar
> 2 tablespoons butter, melted
> 2 teaspoons salt
> 2 packages dry yeast (about 4½ teaspoons)
> 24.2 ounces all-purpose flour (about 5½ cups), divided
> 1 cup chopped walnuts
> 3 tablespoons coarsely chopped fresh rosemary
> 1 large egg, lightly beaten
> Cooking spray
> 1 tablespoon yellow cornmeal
> 1 tablespoon 1% low-fat milk
> 1 large egg, lightly beaten

1. Combine first 5 ingredients in a large bowl, stirring with a whisk. Add yeast, stirring with a whisk; let stand 5 minutes. Weigh or lightly spoon flour into dry measuring cups; level with a knife. Add 9 ounces flour (about 2 cups) to yeast mixture, stirring with a whisk. Cover and let rise in a warm place (85°), free from drafts, 15 minutes.

2. Add 11 ounces flour (about 2½ cups), walnuts, rosemary, and 1 egg, stirring with a whisk. Turn dough out onto a lightly floured surface. Knead until smooth and elastic (about 10 minutes), adding enough of remaining flour, ¼ cup at a time, to prevent dough from sticking to hands.

3. Place dough in a large bowl coated with cooking spray, turning to coat top. Cover and let rise in a warm place (85°), free from drafts, 1 hour or until doubled in size. (Lightly press two fingers into dough; if indentation remains, the dough has risen enough.)

4. Preheat oven to 400°.

5. Punch dough down; turn dough out onto a lightly floured surface. Divide dough in half, shaping each portion into a round. Place loaves on a baking sheet dusted with cornmeal. Cover and let rise 30 minutes or until doubled in size.

6. Combine 1 tablespoon milk and 1 egg, stirring with a whisk; brush over loaves. Make 3 diagonal cuts ¼-inch deep across top of each loaf using a sharp knife.

7. Place loaves in oven; reduce oven temperature to 375°, and bake 40 minutes or until bottom of each loaf sounds hollow when tapped. Let stand 20 minutes before slicing. **Yield: 2 loaves, 12 servings per loaf (serving size: 1 slice).**

CALORIES 170; FAT 5.2g (sat 1.2g, mono 1g, poly 2.6g); PROTEIN 5.2g; CARB 25.7g; FIBER 1.3g; CHOL 21mg; IRON 1.7mg; SODIUM 222mg; CALC 39mg

kitchen how-to:
chop rosemary

Working with 1 fresh rosemary sprig at a time, hold the leafy end of the sprig in one hand, and strip the leaves off the sprig with the other hand. Chop the leaves.

Flaky Dinner Rolls

    3 tablespoons sugar
    1 package dry yeast (about 2¼ teaspoons)
    1 cup warm fat-free milk (100° to 110°)
 13.5 ounces all-purpose flour (about 3 cups),
       divided
    ¾ teaspoon salt
    3 tablespoons butter, softened
   Cooking spray

1. Dissolve sugar and yeast in warm milk in a large bowl; let stand 5 minutes. Weigh or lightly spoon flour into dry measuring cups; level with a knife. Add 2¾ cups flour and salt to yeast mixture; stir until a dough forms. Turn dough out onto a lightly floured surface. Knead until smooth (about 5 minutes); add enough of remaining flour, 1 tablespoon at a time, to prevent dough from sticking to hands (dough will feel slightly sticky). Cover dough with plastic wrap, and let rest for 10 minutes.
2. Roll dough into a 12 x 10–inch rectangle on a lightly floured baking sheet. Gently spread butter over dough. Working with a long side, fold up bottom third of dough. Fold top third of dough over the first fold to form a 12 x 3–inch rectangle. Cover with plastic wrap; place in freezer for 10 minutes.
3. Remove dough from freezer; remove plastic wrap. Roll dough, still on baking sheet (sprinkle on a little more flour, if needed), into a 12 x 10–inch rectangle. Working with a long side, fold up bottom third of dough. Fold top third of dough over the first fold to form a 12 x 3–inch rectangle. Cover with plastic wrap; place in freezer for 10 minutes.
4. Remove dough from freezer; remove plastic wrap. Roll dough, still on baking sheet, into a 12 x 8–inch rectangle. Beginning with a long side, roll up dough jelly-roll fashion; pinch seam to seal (do not seal ends of roll). Cut roll into 12 equal slices. Place slices, cut sides up, in muffin cups coated with cooking spray. Lightly coat tops of dough slices with cooking spray. Cover and let rise in a warm place (85°), free from drafts, 45 minutes or until doubled in size.
5. Preheat oven to 375°.
6. Bake dough at 375° for 20 minutes or until golden brown. Remove from pan, and cool for 5 minutes on a wire rack. Serve rolls warm. **Yield: 12 servings (serving size: 1 roll).**

CALORIES 160; FAT 3.2g (sat 1.5g, mono 1.2g, poly 0.2g); PROTEIN 4.2g; CARB 28.3g; FIBER 1g; CHOL 8mg; IRON 1.7mg; SODIUM 178mg; CALC 25mg

make flaky dinner rolls

You can make this recipe ahead and freeze the rolls.
After baking the rolls, allow them to cool completely. Place the cooled rolls in a large heavy-duty zip-top plastic bag, or wrap them in plastic wrap and then foil. Freeze them for up to one month. Thaw them in the refrigerator or at room temperature. Wrap them in foil, and reheat them at 350° for 10 minutes or until warm.

1. Once the dough has had time to rest, roll it into a 12 x 10–inch rectangle on a lightly floured baking sheet. Gently spread the butter over the dough. Working with a long side, fold up the bottom third of the dough.

2. Fold the top third of dough over the first fold to form a 12 x 3–inch rectangle. Cover it with plastic wrap, and place it in the freezer for 10 minutes.
3. Remove the dough from the freezer; remove the plastic wrap.

Roll the dough, still on the baking sheet, into a 12 x 8–inch rectangle. Beginning with a long side, roll up the dough jelly-roll fashion; pinch the seam to seal (do not seal the ends of the roll). Cut the roll into 12 equal slices. Place the slices, cut

sides up, in muffin cups coated with cooking spray. Lightly coat the tops of the dough slices with cooking spray. Cover and let rise in a warm place (85°), free from drafts, 45 minutes or until doubled in size. Bake.

{vegan recipe}

Moroccan Flatbreads

Serve these alongside soups or salads. You can bake the breadsticks the night before, cool them to room temperature, and store them in an airtight container; serve them at room temperature, or reheat them in the microwave the next day.

½ teaspoon dry yeast
¾ cup plus 1 tablespoon warm water (100° to 110°)
9 ounces all-purpose flour (about 2 cups)
¾ teaspoon sea salt
Cooking spray
2 cups chopped onion
½ cup finely chopped fresh flat-leaf parsley
2 tablespoons extra-virgin olive oil
2 teaspoons paprika
1 teaspoon ground cumin
½ teaspoon sea salt
¼ teaspoon crushed red pepper
1 teaspoon canola oil, divided

1. Dissolve yeast in warm water in a large bowl; let stand 5 minutes. Weigh or lightly spoon flour into dry measuring cups; level with a knife. Add flour and ¾ teaspoon salt to yeast mixture; stir with a wooden spoon until smooth. Turn dough out onto a lightly floured surface; knead 3 minutes. Shape dough into a ball; invert bowl over the dough, and let stand for 15 minutes. Uncover; knead dough 3 minutes. Divide dough into 8 equal portions, shaping each into a ball; lightly coat with cooking spray. Cover with plastic wrap; let stand for 30 minutes.

2. Combine onion and next 6 ingredients in a bowl.

3. Working with one dough portion at a time (cover remaining dough to prevent drying), carefully flatten each portion into a 6½-inch circle (dough will be delicate). Spoon 2 tablespoons onion mixture into center of dough. Fold sides of dough over filling. Fold one short side under dough; fold other short side over dough. Gently press square of dough to seal. Repeat procedure with remaining dough portions and onion mixture.

4. Heat ½ teaspoon oil in a large nonstick skillet over medium heat. Add 4 flatbreads to pan; cook for 2 minutes on each side or until crisp and golden. Transfer flatbreads to a parchment paper-lined platter. Repeat procedure with remaining ½ teaspoon oil and 4 flatbreads. Serve immediately. **Yield: 4 servings (serving size: 2 flatbreads).**

CALORIES 331; FAT 8.9g (sat 1.2g, mono 5.7g, poly 1.3g); PROTEIN 7.8g; CARB 54.5g; FIBER 3.6g; CHOL 0mg; IRON 3.9mg; SODIUM 730mg; CALC 40mg

kitchen how-to: make foolproof flatbreads

Homemade breads are at the heart of Moroccan cuisine and culture. Used as serving utensils to scoop up food at meals, they're also a symbol of hospitality since bread is shared with guests. Carry on this Mediterranean tradition by welcoming diners to your table with Moroccan Flatbreads, substantial enough for an entrée or as a partner for soup or salad. Add cheese or herbs to vary the filling. Follow these steps for working with the dough and shaping the breads.

1. Lightly spray your hands with cooking spray, if needed, to avoid tearing the dough. Carefully flatten each dough portion to a 6½-inch round; the dough will be delicate and very thin at this point.

2. Fold the dough to make a square package. Fold 2 opposite sides over the filling; then fold one short side over the dough and one short side under the dough. Lightly press the square to seal it.

3. Because the dough is tender and thin, it crisps and browns nicely when heated. Carefully turn over the flatbreads when they are golden and slightly crisp on the bottom.

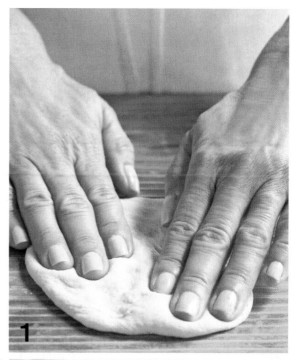

Caramel-Pecan Sticky Buns

You can keep these buns light by trimming the amount of butter traditionally used and using dark brown muscovado sugar, which enhances richness without adding fat. If you don't have dark brown muscovado sugar, these buns are also fantastic with regular dark brown sugar. Chopping the pecans distributes their flavor while allowing you to use fewer nuts.

Caramel:
- ⅓ cup packed dark brown muscovado sugar or dark brown sugar
- 3 tablespoons butter
- 4 teaspoons light corn syrup
- Cooking spray
- 2 tablespoons chopped pecans

Dough:
- 1 package dry yeast (about 2¼ teaspoons)
- 1⅔ cups warm water (100° to 110°)
- 1½ teaspoons salt
- 23.5 ounces all-purpose flour (about 5¼ cups), divided
- ⅓ cup granulated sugar
- 1 teaspoon ground cinnamon
- 2 tablespoons butter, softened

1. To prepare caramel, combine first 3 ingredients in a saucepan over medium heat; stir frequently until butter melts. Continue cooking until mixture thickens and becomes smooth (about 1 minute), stirring constantly. Remove from heat; pour into the center of a 9-inch square baking pan; quickly spread caramel onto pan bottom using a spatula coated with cooking spray. Sprinkle with pecans; cool to room temperature. Lightly coat sides of pan with cooking spray.

2. To prepare dough, dissolve yeast in warm water in a large bowl; let stand 5 minutes. Stir in salt.

3. Weigh or lightly spoon flour into dry measuring cups; level with a knife. Add 5 cups flour to yeast mixture; stir until a soft dough forms. Turn dough out onto a floured surface. Knead until smooth and elastic (about 8 minutes); add enough of remaining flour, 1 tablespoon at a time, to keep dough from sticking to hands.

4. Place dough in a large bowl coated with cooking spray, turning to coat top. Cover and let rise in a warm place (85°), free from drafts, 1 hour or until doubled in size. (Gently press two fingers into dough; if indentation remains, the dough has risen enough.) Punch dough down; cover and let rest 5 minutes.

5. Combine granulated sugar and cinnamon in a small bowl; set aside.

6. Roll dough into a 16 x 12–inch rectangle on a lightly floured surface; spread 2 tablespoons of softened butter over dough. Sprinkle with cinnamon-sugar mixture, leaving a ½-inch border. Roll up rectangle tightly, starting with long edge, pressing firmly to eliminate air pockets; pinch seam to seal (do not seal ends). Cut into 16 (1-inch-wide) slices. Place slices in prepared pan (rolls will be crowded). Cover and let rise 30 minutes or until doubled in size.

7. Preheat oven to 375°.

8. Bake at 375° for 20 minutes or until rolls are light golden brown. Cool in pan 5 minutes on rack. Place a serving platter upside down on top of pan; invert onto platter. Serve warm. **Yield: 16 servings (serving size: 1 roll).**

CALORIES 232; FAT 5.3g (sat 1.9g, mono 2.1g, poly 0.7g); PROTEIN 4.5g; CARB 41.7g; FIBER 1.4g; CHOL 9mg; IRON 2.1mg; SODIUM 249mg; CALC 14mg

kitchen how-to:
arrange sticky buns

Cut the filled roll into 16 (1-inch-wide) slices. Place the slices in prepared pan (rolls will be crowded). Cover and let rise 30 minutes or until doubled in size. Bake.

way to cook vegetarian

grains & pasta

learn how to

grains & pasta

Grains and pastas are filling, satisfying, and amazingly versatile. Cuisines around the world employ the relatively neutral flavor of grains and pastas as the base of many vegetarian meals, mixing them with a variety of vegetables, cheeses, sauces, and seasonings that give new life to each dish.

wild rice

millet

The Importance of Whole Grains

Grains and pastas are a key part of the vegetarian diet, and whole grains are particularly important. A whole grain includes the germ, endosperm, and bran—a trio that provides energy, fiber (which is important in weight loss and maintenance, heart health, and digestion), iron (which can be a concern for nonmeat eaters), zinc, B vitamins, and antioxidants. You'll want to make sure that most (or at least half) of the grains you're eating are whole grains since refined grains (like white bread, white flour, and sugary cereals) lose many of those important nutrients during processing. The glossaries below can help you choose healthy grains and pastas while you explore the wide variety of flavors and textures they offer.

Grains Glossary

With their nutty taste, mild flavor, and irresistible chewy texture, grains make a fitting base for many meals.

Amaranth: Technically not a grain, amaranth is high in protein—and it's a complete protein.
Barley: Its neutral flavor makes barley a great addition to soups or a substitute for Arborio rice in risotto. Barley also contains a specific kind of fiber called beta-glucans (also found in oats), which may help lower levels of total cholesterol, including artery-clogging LDL cholesterol.
Buckwheat: The flavor of buckwheat ranges from nutty to earthy. A ½-cup serving of cooked buckwheat "groats" contains almost 10% of your daily fiber needs.

barley

bulgur

quinoa

Bulgur (cracked wheat): Bulgur consists of wheat kernels that have been precooked, dried, and cut ("cracked"). It has a nutty flavor and can be used in pilafs, soups, and stuffings.

Farro: Also known as emmer, farro is an ancient Italian wheat grain that has a chewy bite. It's often confused with spelt, but they're two distinct grains.

Millet: Millet resembles couscous in texture and has a sweet, nutty flavor.

Quinoa: This small, round, high-protein grain (pronounced KEEN-wah) is an excellent source of iron—it supplies your entire daily recommendation in 1 cup.

Spelt: Higher in protein than more common wheat varieties, spelt provides 12 grams in ½ cup. It's also a good source of fiber.

Wheat berries: This whole-wheat kernel grain has a chewy texture and mild flavor.

Oats Glossary

Whole oats are a tough, chewy grain that have undergone various amounts of cutting, rolling, steaming, and precooking to speed home-preparation time. The good news is that this processing doesn't result in a significant amount of nutrients being lost.

Oat groats: These are oats as nature intended. Similar to wheat berries, groats require about 45 minutes of stovetop simmering before they're tender.

Steel-Cut (Irish): These whole oat groats have been halved or cut into three pieces so they cook faster (in about 20 minutes) and the finished dish is chewier.

Regular (rolled): What most of us know as oatmeal is whole groats that have been steamed and then flattened by large rollers. They cook in about 5 minutes.

Instant: Regular rolled oats have been flattened even more and then cooked and dried. (Don't confuse these with sugary pulverized instant oats that come in packets.)

oat groats

steel-cut (Irish)

regular (rolled)

instant

Rice Glossary

You can find many varieties of rice. Here's a small sample of some of the more widely available types.

1. Brown: This rice has been hulled with the bran intact, and it requires a longer cooking time than other varieties because the bran is a barrier to water.

2. Arborio: This popular Italian rice is used to make risotto. Each medium-length grain has a white "eye" that remains firm to the bite, while the rest of the grain softens and lends creaminess to the dish.

3. Wild: This is the only grain native to North America, though it's actually not a rice at all but the seed from an aquatic grass. Even after cooking, wild rice still has a distinct crunch that makes it an excellent mix-in with more traditional whole grains, such as brown rice.

4. Basmati: This long-grain variety is highly regarded for its fragrance, taste, and slender shape.

5. Parboiled: This tan grain is firm and stays separated when cooked. Don't confuse parboiled rice with instant—parboiled rice takes longer to cook.

Oat and Wheat Bran
What they add: Both are excellent sources of fiber.

Dried Fruit
What it adds: A majority of the water content has been removed from dried fruit, which means it has a concentrated sweet flavor.

Steel-Cut Irish Oats
What it adds: This type of oat provides a chewy texture.

Pan-Seared Oatmeal with Warm Fruit Compote and Cider Syrup

Syrup:
   2 cups apple cider

Compote:
   2 cups water
   ¼ cup packed brown sugar
   ½ teaspoon ground cinnamon
   1 (7-ounce) package dried mixed fruit bits

Oatmeal:
   3 cups water
   1 cup fat-free milk
   ¼ cup packed brown sugar
   ½ teaspoon ground cinnamon
   ¼ teaspoon salt
   1½ cups steel-cut (Irish) oats
   Cooking spray
   ¼ cup butter, divided

1. To prepare syrup, bring cider to a boil in a small saucepan over medium-high heat. Cook until reduced to ⅓ cup (about 20 minutes); set aside.
2. To prepare compote, combine 2 cups water, ¼ cup sugar, ½ teaspoon cinnamon, and dried fruit in a medium saucepan; bring to a boil. Reduce heat, and simmer 20 minutes or until thick.
3. To prepare oatmeal, combine 3 cups water, 1 cup milk, ¼ cup brown sugar, ½ teaspoon cinnamon, and salt in a large saucepan. Bring to a boil over medium-high heat; stir in oats. Reduce heat; simmer 20 minutes or until thick, stirring occasionally. Spoon oatmeal into an 11 x 7–inch baking dish coated with cooking spray; cool to room temperature. Cover and chill at least 1 hour or until set.
4. Invert chilled oatmeal mixture onto a cutting board. Using a sharp knife, cut oatmeal into 8 equal rectangles; cut each rectangle in half diagonally to form 16 triangles.
5. Melt 2 tablespoons butter in a large nonstick skillet over medium heat. Add 8 oatmeal triangles; cook 3 minutes on each side or until golden brown. Remove from pan; keep warm. Repeat procedure with remaining 2 tablespoons butter and oatmeal triangles. Place 2 oatmeal triangles on each of 8 plates, and top each serving with 3½ tablespoons fruit compote and about 2 teaspoons syrup. **Yield: 8 servings.**

CALORIES 314; FAT 7.9g (sat 3.9g, mono 2.3g, poly 0.9g); PROTEIN 5.8g; CARB 58.7g; FIBER 2.8g; CHOL 16mg; IRON 2.4mg; SODIUM 167mg; CALC 76mg

kitchen how-to:
make pan-seared oatmeal

1

2

Pan-seared oatmeal is easy to get excited about—hearty oats are chilled and cut into triangles and then seared in butter. You can top them with warm fruit, fresh berries, and syrup. All of the components can be made a day ahead and reheated.

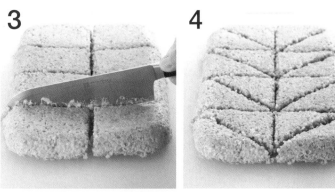

3   **4**

1. Prepare the oatmeal mixture, and spoon it into an 11 x 7–inch baking dish coated with cooking spray; let it cool to room temperature.

2. Cover and chill the oatmeal mixture for at least 1 hour or until set.

3. Invert the chilled oatmeal mixture onto a cutting board. Using a sharp knife, cut the oatmeal into 8 equal rectangles.

4. Cut each rectangle in half diagonally to form 16 triangles.

5. Melt 2 tablespoons butter in a large nonstick skillet over medium heat. Add 8 oatmeal triangles; cook 3 minutes on each side or until golden brown. Remove the oatmeal triangles from pan; keep warm. Repeat the procedure with remaining butter and oatmeal triangles.

5

grains

In addition to their numerous health benefits, grains are satisfying. Their nuttiness and chewiness bring more to the table than just healthy food.

Farro Risotto with Mushrooms

- 1 cup dried wild mushroom blend (about 1 ounce)
- 5½ cups Mushroom Stock or organic vegetable broth
- 2 tablespoons extra-virgin olive oil
- 1½ cups uncooked farro
- ½ cup finely chopped onion
- 2 garlic cloves, minced
- 6 cups sliced cremini mushrooms (about 1 pound)
- ¾ teaspoon salt, divided
- ½ cup dry white wine
- 1 teaspoon chopped fresh thyme
- ¼ cup (1 ounce) grated fresh Parmigiano-Reggiano cheese
- ¼ cup chopped fresh flat-leaf parsley
- ½ teaspoon freshly ground black pepper

1. Place dried mushrooms in a medium bowl; cover with boiling water. Let stand 30 minutes or until tender; drain. Coarsely chop mushrooms.
2. Bring Mushroom Stock to a simmer in a small saucepan (do not boil). Keep stock warm over low heat.

3. Heat a Dutch oven over medium heat. Add oil to pan; swirl to coat. Add farro and onion; cook 5 minutes, stirring occasionally. Add garlic; cook 1 minute, stirring constantly. Add rehydrated mushrooms, cremini mushrooms, and ½ teaspoon salt; sauté 5 minutes or until cremini mushrooms are tender, stirring occasionally. Add wine and thyme; cook until liquid almost evaporates.

4. Add ½ cup stock to farro mixture; cook over medium heat 4 minutes or until the liquid is nearly absorbed, stirring occasionally. Add 4½ cups stock, ½ cup at a time, stirring occasionally until each portion of stock is absorbed before adding the next (about 40 minutes total).

5. Add remaining ¼ teaspoon salt, ½ cup stock, cheese, parsley, and pepper; stir until cheese melts. **Yield: 6 servings (serving size: 1 cup).**

CALORIES 271; FAT 7.1g (sat 1.7g, mono 3.9g, poly 1g); PROTEIN 12.2g; CARB 43.4g; FIBER 8.5g; CHOL 4mg; IRON 1.8mg; SODIUM 378mg; CALC 71mg

Mushroom Stock

2	cups boiling water
½	cup dried porcini mushrooms (about ½ ounce)
1	whole garlic head
1	tablespoon extra-virgin olive oil
2	cups (1-inch) slices onion
2	cups (1-inch) slices leek
1	pound cremini mushrooms, quartered
4	parsley sprigs
4	thyme sprigs
10	black peppercorns
1	bay leaf
¼	cup dry white wine
6½	cups water

1. Combine 2 cups boiling water and porcini mushrooms in a bowl. Cover and let stand 30 minutes or until tender. Strain through a fine sieve over a bowl; reserve 1½ cups liquid and mushrooms.

2. Cut off pointed end of garlic just to expose cloves; set aside.

3. Heat a Dutch oven over medium-high heat. Add oil to pan; swirl to coat. Add onion and leek; sauté 5 minutes or until tender, stirring occasionally. Add porcini mushrooms, garlic, cremini mushrooms, and next 4 ingredients; sauté 10 minutes or until cremini mushrooms are tender, stirring occasionally. Add wine; cook until liquid evaporates (about 2 minutes). Add reserved 1½ cups mushroom liquid and 6½ cups water; bring to a boil. Reduce heat, and simmer 50 minutes. Strain through fine sieve over a bowl; discard solids. Store in an airtight container in the refrigerator up to 1 week. **Yield: 6 servings (serving size: 1 cup).**

CALORIES 28; FAT 2.4g (sat 0.3g, mono 1.7g, poly 0.3g); PROTEIN 0.5g; CARB 1.6g; FIBER 0.3g; CHOL 0mg; IRON 0.2mg; SODIUM 3mg; CALC 5mg

kitchen how-to: reconstitute dried mushrooms

The best varieties of mushrooms to use in dried form are porcini, shiitake, and morel, although many other kinds also pack a flavorful punch. When mushrooms are dried, they shrivel, and their flavor concentrates. Look inside the package of dried mushrooms before you buy them to see how big the pieces are; if they've crumbled to dust, don't buy them.

1. Place the dried mushrooms in a bowl; cover the mushrooms with boiling water or other liquid, such as broth.

2. Let the mushrooms stand in the boiling water for 30 minutes or until tender; drain them in a fine sieve placed over a bowl. The liquid drained from the mushrooms is very flavorful; reserve it for use as a sauce, if you'd like.

{vegan recipe}
Southwestern Barley "Grits"

This savory cereal—imagine cheese grits infused with chiles—will take the chill off the coldest mornings.

1¼ cups uncooked pearl barley
3 cups water
3 cups 1% low-fat milk
1 tablespoon honey
¾ teaspoon salt
1 cup (4 ounces) shredded sharp cheddar cheese
1 teaspoon chili powder
1 (4.5-ounce) can chopped green chiles, drained
6 tablespoons reduced-fat sour cream
Hot sauce (optional)

1. Place ⅓ cup barley in a blender; process until coarsely ground (about 15 to 20 seconds). Place ground barley in a large saucepan. Repeat procedure with remaining barley. Cook barley over medium heat 4 minutes or until toasted, stirring frequently.
2. Add water, milk, honey, and salt; bring to a boil. Reduce heat; simmer 25 minutes or until barley is soft, stirring frequently. Add cheese, chili powder, and chiles; cook 5 minutes or until cheese melts, stirring constantly. Top each serving with 1 tablespoon sour cream. Serve with hot sauce, if desired.
Yield: 6 servings (serving size: 1 cup).

CALORIES 314; FAT 10g (sat 6.1g, mono 2.2g, poly 0.5g); PROTEIN 13.8g; CARB 43.7g; FIBER 6.9g; CHOL 32mg; IRON 1.4mg; SODIUM 739mg; CALC 327mg

kitchen how-to: toast barley

Grinding the barley cracks the grains, which allows them to cook faster and maintains their chewy texture. Toasting the grains brings out their flavor. If you like, you can grind and toast the barley ahead of time and store it in an airtight container.

1. Place the barley in a blender, and process it until it's coarsely ground (about 15 to 20 seconds).
2. Place the ground barley in a large saucepan.
3. Cook the ground barley over medium heat for 4 minutes or until toasted—it will become a rich brown. Stir the barley frequently so it browns evenly and doesn't burn.

{vegan recipe}
Quinoa with Leeks and Shiitake Mushrooms

Quinoa, which is high in protein and iron, takes only 15 minutes to cook. Serve this tasty dish with sautéed soy "sausage" links.

2	cups organic vegetable broth
1	cup water
½	teaspoon salt, divided
1½	cups uncooked quinoa, rinsed
3	tablespoons chopped fresh flat-leaf parsley
1	tablespoon olive oil, divided
¼	teaspoon freshly ground black pepper, divided
3	cups thinly sliced leeks (about 2 large)
4	cups thinly sliced shiitake mushroom caps (about 8 ounces)
1½	cups chopped red bell pepper
¼	cup dry white wine
½	cup coarsely chopped walnuts

1. Combine broth, water, and ¼ teaspoon salt in a large saucepan; bring to a boil. Stir in quinoa. Cover, reduce heat, and simmer 15 minutes or until liquid is absorbed. Stir in parsley, 1½ teaspoons oil, and ⅛ teaspoon black pepper. Remove from heat; keep warm.
2. Heat remaining 1½ teaspoons oil in a medium nonstick skillet over medium-high heat. Add leeks; sauté 6 minutes or until wilted. Add mushroom caps, bell pepper, and wine; cook 2 minutes or until vegetables are tender. Stir in remaining ¼ teaspoon salt and remaining ⅛ teaspoon black pepper. Place 1 cup quinoa mixture in each of 4 shallow bowls; top each with 1¼ cups vegetable mixture and 2 tablespoons walnuts. **Yield: 4 servings.**

CALORIES 495; FAT 15.7g (sat 1.7g, mono 5.7g, poly 6.2g); PROTEIN 15.8g; CARB 73.8g; FIBER 7.9g; CHOL 0mg; IRON 10.5mg; SODIUM 839mg; CALC 95mg

{ vegan recipe }

Bulgur with Dried Cranberries

1 cup coarse-ground bulgur
2 cups boiling water
2 cups (¼-inch) cubed peeled English cucumber
1 cup dried cranberries
1 cup finely chopped fresh flat-leaf parsley
⅓ cup thinly sliced green onion
1 teaspoon grated lemon rind
⅓ cup fresh lemon juice
⅓ cup extra-virgin olive oil
¾ teaspoon kosher salt
¾ teaspoon freshly ground black pepper

1. Place bulgur in a large bowl; cover with 2 cups boiling water. Cover; let stand 30 minutes or until liquid is absorbed. Fluff with a fork. Add cucumber and remaining ingredients; toss gently to combine.

Yield: 8 servings (serving size: 1 cup).

CALORIES 197; FAT 9.6g (sat 1.3g, mono 6.7g, poly 1.2g); PROTEIN 2.7g; CARB 28.2g; FIBER 4.7g; CHOL 0mg; IRON 1.2mg; SODIUM 186mg; CALC 27mg

rice

Rice pairs nicely with all types of food and can easily be incorporated into any part of a meal.

{vegan recipe}
Koshari

This Egyptian street food is a starch-lover's dream: Rice, pasta, and legumes crowned with a spicy-sweet tomato sauce and creamy caramelized onions.

Sauce:

 1 tablespoon extra-virgin olive oil
 1 cup finely chopped onion
 1½ tablespoons minced garlic
 ½ teaspoon sea salt
 ½ teaspoon freshly ground black pepper
 ½ teaspoon crushed red pepper
 2 (14.5-ounce) cans diced tomatoes, undrained

Koshari:

 3 tablespoons extra-virgin olive oil
 3 cups thinly sliced onion
 ½ cup uncooked vermicelli, broken into 1-inch pieces
 5 cups water
 1¼ cups dried lentils or yellow split peas
 2½ cups hot cooked long-grain rice
 1 teaspoon sea salt

1. To prepare sauce, heat 1 tablespoon oil in a large saucepan over medium heat. Add chopped onion to pan, and cook 15 minutes or until golden, stirring occasionally. Add garlic; cook 2 minutes. Stir in ½ teaspoon salt, peppers, and

kitchen how-to: make basic rice

To make perfect rice every time, select a broad saucepan, deep skillet, or sauté pan with a snug-fitting lid.

1. For 1 cup of uncooked rice, bring 2 cups of water to a boil in a medium saucepan. Add the rice. Cover, reduce heat, and simmer 18 minutes or until the liquid is absorbed and the rice is done. Do not lift the lid or stir while the rice is cooking. Lifting the lid allows steam to escape, and stirring the rice will release more starch, causing the grains to stick together in lumps.
2. Remove the pan from the heat, and let the rice stand for 5 to 10 minutes. Uncover the pan carefully—try not to let the condensation on the lid drip onto the rice. Fluff the rice with a fork.

tomatoes; cook 10 minutes or until slightly thick. Transfer tomato mixture to a food processor; process 1 minute or until smooth. Keep warm. Wipe skillet dry with paper towels.
2. To prepare koshari, heat 3 tablespoons oil in pan over medium heat. Add sliced onion; cook 15 minutes or until deep golden brown, stirring frequently. Remove onion with a slotted spoon to several layers of paper towels; set aside. Return pan to medium heat. Add vermicelli; sauté 2 minutes or until golden brown, stirring frequently. Set aside.
3. Combine 5 cups water and lentils in a medium saucepan; bring

to a boil. Cover, reduce heat, and simmer 30 minutes or until lentils are tender. Remove from heat; add vermicelli, stirring well to combine. Wrap a clean kitchen towel around lid, and cover lentil mixture; let stand 10 minutes or until vermicelli is tender. Add rice and 1 teaspoon salt to lentil mixture; fluff with a fork. Serve immediately with sauce and onions. **Yield: 8 servings (serving size: ¾ cup lentil mixture, ⅓ cup sauce, and 2 tablespoons onion mixture).**

CALORIES 292; FAT 7.7g (sat 1g, mono 5g, poly 0.8g); PROTEIN 10.2g; CARB 47.5g; FIBER 7.6g; CHOL 0mg; IRON 3mg; SODIUM 569mg; CALC 53mg

Meatless Brown Rice–Stuffed Peppers

- 4 large green bell peppers
- ¼ teaspoon salt
- Cooking spray
- ½ cup chopped onion
- 2 garlic cloves, minced
- 1 jalapeño pepper, minced
- 2 cups tomato-basil pasta sauce, divided
- ½ cup (2 ounces) grated fresh Parmesan cheese, divided
- ¼ teaspoon freshly ground black pepper
- 2 (8.8-ounce) packages precooked brown rice (such as Uncle Ben's Ready Rice)
- 1 (12-ounce) package frozen meatless crumbles (such as Morning Star Farms)

1. Preheat oven to 400°.

2. Cut bell peppers in half lengthwise; discard seeds and membranes, leaving stems intact. Place pepper halves, cut sides down, on a large microwave-safe plate; cover with wax paper. Microwave at HIGH 5 minutes. Place pepper halves, cut sides up, on a foil-lined jelly-roll pan. Sprinkle pepper halves with salt.

3. While pepper halves cook, heat a large nonstick skillet over medium-high heat. Coat pan with cooking spray. Add onion, garlic, and jalapeño to pan; sauté 5 minutes or until onion is lightly browned.

4. Combine onion mixture, 1 cup pasta sauce, ¼ cup cheese, and remaining 3 ingredients in a large bowl, stirring until blended. Spoon rice mixture into pepper halves. Spoon remaining 1 cup pasta sauce evenly over tops of peppers.

5. Cover and bake at 400° for 20 minutes. Uncover and sprinkle with remaining ¼ cup cheese. Bake an additional 3 minutes or until cheese melts. **Yield: 4 servings (serving size: 2 stuffed pepper halves).**

CALORIES 344; FAT 5.3g (sat 0.9g, mono 0.8g, poly 1.8g); PROTEIN 16.3g; CARB 58.6g; FIBER 5.8g; CHOL 4mg; IRON 2.9mg; SODIUM 557mg; CALC 117mg

kitchen how-to: make tofu fried rice

Traditionally, the caramel tint of fried rice comes from cooking foods in very hot oil and then adding a soy-heavy seasoning sauce. Here we use a blend of soy sauce, sake, hoisin sauce, and a bit of sesame oil without overdoing the sodium. We also ration the oil to curb calories.

1. Cook the rice according to the package directions, omitting the salt and fat. Sauté the tofu in 1 tablespoon vegetable oil until it's browned to add richness and color to the dish. The protein content of tofu makes this a main dish, but you can omit it to keep this fried rice as a side dish. Remove the tofu from the pan, and add the eggs. Cook the eggs 1 minute or until done, breaking the egg into small pieces. Remove the egg from the pan.
2. Add 1 tablespoon of vegetable oil to the pan. Add the onions, peas and carrots, garlic, and ginger; sauté 2 minutes.

3. While the vegetable mixture cooks, combine the sake, soy sauce, hoisin sauce, and sesame oil. Add the cooked rice to the pan; cook 2 minutes, stirring constantly.

4. Add the tofu, egg, and soy sauce mixture; cook 30 seconds, stirring constantly. Garnish this dish with sliced green onions, if you'd like.

{vegan recipe}

Vegetable Maki

Sushi:
- 5 cups Basic Japanese White Rice
- 2 tablespoons rice vinegar
- 2 teaspoons sugar
- ½ teaspoon kosher salt
- 1 cup finely chopped fresh shiitake mushrooms (about 2½ ounces)
- ½ cup finely chopped carrot
- 2 tablespoons sesame seeds, toasted
- 1 tablespoon less-sodium soy sauce
- 1 tablespoon mirin (sweet rice wine)
- 6 nori (seaweed) sheets

Ponzu Sauce:
- ¼ cup less-sodium soy sauce
- 2 tablespoons fresh orange juice
- 1 tablespoon fresh lemon juice
- 1½ teaspoons water
- 1½ teaspoons mirin (sweet rice wine)
- Dash of crushed red pepper

1. To prepare sushi, place Basic Japanese White Rice in a bowl. Combine vinegar, sugar, and salt; sprinkle over rice, tossing gently with a wooden spoon.

2. Combine shiitake mushrooms and next 4 ingredients in a small bowl; set aside.

3. Cut off top quarter of each nori sheet along short end. Place 1 nori sheet, shiny side down, on a sushi mat covered with plastic wrap, with the long end toward you. Pat about ¾ cup rice mixture evenly over nori with moist hands, leaving a 1-inch border on 1 long end of nori. Sprinkle about 3 tablespoons mushroom mixture over rice. Lift edge of nori closest to you; fold over filling. Lift bottom edge of sushi mat; roll toward top edge, pressing firmly on sushi roll. Continue rolling to top edge; press mat to seal sushi roll. Let rest, seam side down, 5 minutes. Slice about ½-inch from each end of roll; discard trimmings. Slice roll crosswise into 5 pieces. Repeat procedure with remaining nori, rice, and mushroom mixture.

4. To prepare ponzu sauce, combine soy sauce and remaining ingredients in a bowl. Cover and chill until ready to serve. Serve sushi with sauce.

Yield: 6 servings (serving size: 5 maki pieces and about 1 tablespoon sauce).

CALORIES 254; FAT 1.7g (sat 0.1g, mono 0.1g, poly 0.1g); PROTEIN 5.2g; CARB 51.4g; FIBER 2.1g; CHOL 0mg; IRON 2.8mg; SODIUM 522mg; CALC 9mg

Basic Japanese White Rice

Perfect Japanese rice is pearly white and sticky enough to pick up with chopsticks. The initial rinsing process rids the grains of the powdered bran and polishing compound and also plumps them with water to render them tender and delicious.

1½ **cups uncooked short-grain rice (sushi rice)**
1¾ **cups water**

1. Place rice in a fine mesh strainer. Rinse under cold running water, gently stirring rice until water runs clear (about 1 minute).
2. Combine rice and 1¾ cups water in a heavy medium saucepan; let stand 1 hour. Bring to a boil; cover, reduce heat, and simmer 10 minutes. Remove from heat. Let stand, covered, 10 minutes. **Yield: 5 servings (serving size: 1 cup).**

CALORIES 215; FAT 0.3g (sat 0.1g, mono 0.1g, poly 0.1g); PROTEIN 3.9g; CARB 47.5g; FIBER 1.7g; CHOL 0mg; IRON 2.5mg; SODIUM 1mg; CALC 2mg

kitchen how-to:
roll maki

Maki (rice rolled in nori) are easy to prepare once you master the rolling technique. Most Japanese markets sell bamboo rolling mats.

1. Moisten your hands in a bowl of equal parts water and rice vinegar before pressing the sticky rice onto the nori.
2. Cut off the top quarter of each nori sheet along the short end. Place 1 nori sheet, shiny side down, on a sushi mat covered with plastic wrap, with the long end toward you. Pat the sticky rice mixture evenly over the nori, leaving a 1-inch border on 1 long end of the nori. Sprinkle the filling over the rice.
3. Lift the edge of the nori closest to you; fold it over the filling. Lift the bottom edge of the sushi mat; roll it toward the top edge, pressing firmly on the sushi roll.
4. Continue rolling the nori to the top edge; press the sushi mat to seal the roll. Let it rest, seam side down, 5 minutes.
5. Slice about ½ inch from each end of the roll; discard the trimmings. Slice the roll crosswise into 5 pieces.

Sweet Pea Risotto with Corn Broth

Corn Broth:
2½ cups water
2 cups fresh corn kernels
¼ teaspoon salt

Risotto:
3 cups organic vegetable broth (such as Swanson Certified Organic)
2 tablespoons butter
1 cup uncooked Arborio rice
½ cup diced onion
3 tablespoons minced carrot
3 tablespoons minced celery
2 cups fresh green peas
1 cup fresh corn kernels
½ cup diced fresh fennel
2 tablespoons grated Parmesan cheese
2 teaspoons chopped fresh thyme

Remaining Ingredients:
1 tablespoon sherry vinegar
1 tablespoon olive oil
1 teaspoon sugar
¼ teaspoon salt
1 garlic clove, minced
2 tablespoons grated Parmesan cheese
1 tablespoon chopped fresh parsley
1 tablespoon chopped fresh chives

1. To prepare corn broth, combine 2½ cups water and 2 cups corn kernels in a small saucepan; bring to a boil. Reduce heat, and simmer 5 minutes or until corn is tender. Stir in ¼ teaspoon salt. Place corn mixture in blender; process until smooth. Strain corn mixture through a sieve into a bowl; discard solids. Set aside; keep warm.

2. To prepare risotto, bring vegetable broth to a simmer in a medium saucepan (do not boil); keep warm over low heat. Heat butter in a large saucepan over medium-high heat. Add rice; cook 1 minute, stirring constantly. Add onion, carrot, and celery; cook 3 minutes, stirring constantly. Add warm broth, ½ cup at a time, stirring constantly until each portion of broth is absorbed before adding the next (about 20 minutes). Add peas, 1 cup corn kernels, fennel, 2 tablespoons cheese, and thyme, stirring until blended and hot. Keep warm.

3. Combine vinegar, oil, sugar, ¼ teaspoon salt, and garlic in a small bowl, stirring with a whisk until blended. Place about ⅓ cup corn broth into each of 6 bowls. Top each serving with about 1½ cups risotto; drizzle with 1 teaspoon vinaigrette. Sprinkle each serving with 1 teaspoon cheese, ½ teaspoon parsley, and ½ teaspoon chives. Serve immediately. **Yield: 6 servings.**

CALORIES 250; FAT 8.2g (sat 3g, mono 3.9g, poly 0.9g); PROTEIN 7.8g; CARB 38.9g; FIBER 5.3g; CHOL 13mg; IRON 1.5mg; SODIUM 582mg; CALC 65mg

kitchen how-to:
thaw frozen peas

Green peas add fiber, color, and a slightly sweet snap to each bite of this dish. Buying frozen peas saves time and allows you to enjoy their fresh flavor year-round. A quick rinse under cold running water is all that's needed to thaw the frozen peas. Of course, if you happen to find some freshly shelled peas, feel free to substitute them for the frozen ones.

seitan

Seitan makes a great base for vegetarian dishes because it's high in protein—a 4-ounce serving contains 24 grams.

{vegan recipe}
Seitan Stir-Fry with Black Bean Garlic Sauce

Black bean garlic sauce is sold in the international section of some supermarkets and in Asian markets.

- 2 cups boiling water
- 1 ounce dried shiitake mushrooms
- 2 tablespoons Chinese rice wine or sake
- 2 tablespoons black bean garlic sauce (such as Lee Kum Kee)
- 2 teaspoons cornstarch
- 2 tablespoons canola oil, divided
- 2 cups thinly sliced drained seitan (about 8 ounces)
- 1 tablespoon finely chopped garlic
- 1 tablespoon finely chopped peeled fresh ginger
- 4 cups (2-inch) cut green beans (about 1 pound)
- 2 cups hot cooked brown rice
- ¼ teaspoon salt
- Cilantro sprigs (optional)

1. Combine 2 cups boiling water and mushrooms in a small bowl; cover and let stand 20 minutes. Drain in a colander over a bowl, reserving ½ cup soaking liquid. Rinse mushrooms; drain well. Discard mushroom stems; thinly slice mushroom caps.
2. Combine reserved liquid, rice wine, black bean garlic sauce, and cornstarch in a small bowl; stir with a whisk, and set mixture aside.
3. Heat 1 tablespoon canola oil in a large nonstick skillet or wok over medium-high heat. Add seitan to pan, and stir-fry 2 minutes or until lightly browned. Place seitan in a medium bowl. Heat remaining 1 tablespoon oil in pan over medium-high heat. Add garlic and ginger to pan; stir-fry 30 seconds. Add mushrooms and green beans; cover and cook 3 minutes. Add black bean garlic sauce mixture to pan; cook 1 minute or until sauce slightly thickens. Add seitan to pan; cook 1 minute, stirring occasionally. Combine rice and salt; serve seitan mixture over rice. Garnish with cilantro sprigs, if desired. **Yield: 4 servings (serving size: about 1½ cups seitan stir-fry and ½ cup rice).**

CALORIES 474; FAT 10g (sat 0.8g, mono 4.6g, poly 3.5g); PROTEIN 35.5g; CARB 60.7g; FIBER 9.9g; CHOL 0mg; IRON 5.3mg; SODIUM 818mg; CALC 57mg

all about seitan

Although seitan is made from wheat, it has very little in common with bread or flour. Made from wheat gluten (and labeled that way), seitan takes on a meaty texture when it's cooked. Look for it in Asian markets or the refrigerated sections of health food or specialty stores.

pasta

While pasta is both comforting and satisfying, it's most redeeming qualities might be how versatile and affordable it is. You can find it as the base of an Asian-inspired meal or part of a creamy pasta or a delicious lasagna. Regardless, pasta is always a pleaser.

kitchen how-to: cook perfect pasta

If you can boil water, you can make great pasta-based dishes. Most packages give directions, but here are some additional tips. Use a Dutch oven or a stockpot to allow room for the pasta to move freely in the boiling water and cook evenly. You'll want to use as much water as possible.

For 8 ounces of dried pasta, use 4 quarts of water.

1. Fill the pot with water, cover, and bring the water to a full rolling boil over high heat before adding the pasta. It isn't necessary to add salt (for flavor) or oil (to prevent the pasta from sticking) to the water, so omit them to avoid adding sodium and fat.

2. Add the pasta, and start timing the cooking when the water returns to a rolling boil. If you use fresh pasta, remember that it cooks more quickly than dried. After adding pasta to boiling water, put the lid on the pot, but prop it open slightly with a wooden spoon so the water doesn't boil over.

3. Start testing the pasta for doneness a few minutes before the end of the indicated cooking time. Pasta that offers resistance to the bite but has no trace of brittleness is al dente, and that's how you want it. If an under-cooked piece of pasta is cut in half, a white dot or line is clearly visible in the center. Al dente pasta has only a speck of white remaining, meaning the pasta has absorbed just enough water to hydrate it. Drain the cooked pasta in a colander, and shake it well to remove the excess water.

4. If you plan on using the pasta in a salad or filling it, such as in stuffed manicotti shells, rinse the pasta with cold running water. This removes the light coating of starch that covers cooked pasta.

1

2

3

4

Tomato-Ricotta Spaghetti

Roasting tomatoes intensifies their sweetness.
We also tested this recipe with grated Parmigiano-
Reggiano—it's a splurge that makes the difference.

- 2 pints cherry tomatoes, halved (about 4 cups)
- 5 teaspoons extra-virgin olive oil, divided
- ½ teaspoon salt, divided
- 8 ounces uncooked spaghetti
- ⅓ cup chopped fresh basil
- ¼ teaspoon freshly ground black pepper
- ½ cup (2 ounces) ricotta salata cheese, crumbled

1. Preheat oven to 400°.
2. Place tomatoes on a foil-lined baking sheet. Drizzle
with 1 teaspoon oil; sprinkle with ⅛ teaspoon salt. Bake
at 400° for 20 minutes or until tomatoes collapse.
3. Cook pasta according to package directions, omitting
salt and fat. Drain pasta in a colander over a bowl, reserving ⅓ cup cooking liquid. Return pasta and reserved
liquid to pan; stir in tomatoes, remaining 4 teaspoons
oil, remaining ⅜ teaspoon salt, basil, pepper, and
cheese. Toss well. Serve immediately. **Yield:
4 servings (serving size: 1¼ cups).**

CALORIES 314; FAT 8.4g (sat 1.8g, mono 4.7g, poly 1.4g);
PROTEIN 10.5g; CARB 50.3g; FIBER 3.6g; CHOL 4.6mg;
IRON 2.7mg; SODIUM 331mg; CALC 66mg

kitchen how-to:
make a silky smooth cheese sauce

The secret to sublime cheese and pasta dishes is a smooth, creamy cheese sauce. Here are our tips to stir up a perfect sauce every time. Once you've mastered the sauce, get creative—try spooning the cheesy pasta mixture into a casserole dish and broiling it until golden; stir in tomatoes, green onions, roasted bell peppers, grilled eggplant, or any of your favorite vegetables, and top the mixture with buttery fresh breadcrumbs, extra cheese, or a mixture of the two before baking it. The options are endless.

2

3

1. Heavy sauces are often based on a roux made of butter and flour, but our recipes use butter judiciously in order to keep the saturated fat in check. That's why our cheese sauces start by combining flour with a small amount of milk, a mixture known as a slurry. Be sure to stir the slurry with a whisk until it's smooth—lumps are your enemy.

2. Combine the slurry and the remaining milk in a saucepan, and bring the mixture to a boil over medium heat. Cook until the sauce thickens and coats the back of a spoon, stirring constantly with a whisk. Temperature is crucial to a successful sauce. If the cheese gets too hot, the sauce can curdle or develop a grainy texture. Moderate heat and constant stirring will help you avoid scorching the milk.

3. Moist, semisoft cheeses, such as mozzarella or Monterey Jack, usually melt easily, but be careful when working with low-moisture semifirm, firm, or aged cheese like cheddar or Gruyère. These cheeses don't melt easily or smoothly, especially in lower-fat recipes, so you'll need to finely shred them so they'll melt quickly. Be sure the mixture you are adding them to is not above 155° so the cheese melts without separating. Once the sauce is stable, focus on the flavor: Stir in salt, pepper, and additional ingredients such as hot sauce, vegetables, or herbs, and taste for balance. Remember to work quickly, and add the hot pasta to the sauce so you can bake or serve it before it has time to seize.

Baked Vegetable Lasagna

To help ensure that the cheesy layer remains moist and creamy, don't press out the extra water from the tofu. Serve the lasagna with breadsticks and a green salad.

    3   tablespoons olive oil, divided
    ½   cup chopped white onion
    2   garlic cloves, minced
    1   teaspoon kosher salt, divided
    1   teaspoon sugar
    ¼   teaspoon freshly ground black pepper, divided
    ¼   teaspoon crushed red pepper
    1   (28-ounce) can crushed tomatoes
    ½   cup chopped fresh basil
    1   tablespoon chopped fresh oregano
    1   cup ricotta cheese
    ½   cup (2 ounces) grated fresh Parmigiano-
        Reggiano cheese
    1   (14-ounce) package water-packed firm tofu,
        drained
    1   large egg, lightly beaten
    ½   cup thinly sliced green onions
    3   cups finely chopped red bell pepper (about
        2 medium)
    2   medium zucchini, quartered lengthwise and
        thinly sliced (about 3 cups)
    ⅓   cup finely chopped fresh parsley
        Cooking spray
    12 cooked lasagna noodles
    ¾   cup (3 ounces) shredded part-skim mozzarella
        cheese

1. Preheat oven to 375°.
2. Heat 2 tablespoons oil in a medium saucepan over medium-high heat. Add white onion; sauté 5 minutes or until tender. Add garlic; sauté 1 minute or until golden. Add ½ teaspoon salt, sugar, ⅛ teaspoon black pepper, crushed red pepper, and tomatoes. Cover, reduce heat to low, and simmer 15 minutes or until thoroughly heated. Remove from heat; stir in basil and oregano. Cool.
3. Combine ricotta, Parmigiano-Reggiano, tofu, egg, and ¼ teaspoon salt in a food processor; process 10

seconds or until blended. Stir in green onions. Set aside.
4. Heat remaining 1 tablespoon olive oil in a large nonstick skillet over medium-high heat. Add bell pepper, zucchini, and remaining ¼ teaspoon salt to pan; sauté 10 minutes or until vegetables are tender and liquid evaporates. Remove from heat; stir in parsley and remaining ⅛ teaspoon black pepper.
5. Spread ½ cup tomato mixture in bottom of a 13 x 9–inch baking dish coated with cooking spray; top with 3 noodles. Spread ¾ cup tomato mixture over noodles; top with 1 cup tofu mixture and 1 cup zucchini mixture. Repeat layers twice, ending with noodles. Spread remaining ¾ cup tomato mixture over top. Bake at 375° for 35 minutes or until bubbly; top with mozzarella cheese. Bake an additional 5 minutes or until cheese melts. Let stand 10 minutes. **Yield: 8 servings (serving size: 1 piece).**

CALORIES 347; FAT 18g (sat 6.2g, mono 7g, poly 3.6g); PROTEIN 21.6g; CARB 28.8g; FIBER 5.3g; CHOL 53mg; IRON 8.1mg; SODIUM 543mg; CALC 595mg

kitchen how-to:
assemble baked lasagna

Lasagna is comforting, rich, and easy to assemble. You can sandwich virtually any kind of filling between those sheets of pasta: beans, eggplant, artichoke hearts, a mixture of vegetables, cheese—you name it. And lasagna is an ideal make-ahead entrée.

1. Spread ½ cup of the tomato mixture across the bottom of a 13 x 9–inch baking dish coated with cooking spray. This should be a thin layer.
2. Top the tomato mixture with 3 noodles.
3. Spread ¾ cup of the tomato mixture over the noodles.
4. Top the noodles and sauce with 1 cup of the tofu mixture and 1 cup of the zucchini mixture.
5. Repeat the layers twice, ending with noodles. Spread the remaining ¾ cup of the tomato mixture over top. Bake the lasagna according to the recipe directions.

Lo Mein Egg Noodles

What they add: Malaysian food is a melting pot of flavors and traditions. Chinese lo mein egg noodles star in this spicy stir-fry—their dramatic length and chunky texture make them perfect for the thick sauce.

Baby Bok Choy

What it adds: The sautéed bok choy adds a slight crunch, and its little green leaves perk up the color of this popular dish.

Dried Porcinis

What they add: The dried porcini mushrooms add a rich earthiness to this dish. Plus, the flavorful porcini soaking liquid provides the foundation for a rich sauce.

Truffle Oil

What it adds: This oil adds an intense earthy flavor and a pungent aroma. A little bit can go a long way.

Bucatini with Mushrooms

1/2	cup dried porcini mushrooms (about 1/2 ounce)
2/3	cup boiling water
8	ounces uncooked bucatini
3 1/2	teaspoons salt, divided
1	tablespoon butter
1/4	cup finely chopped shallots
2	(4-ounce) packages exotic mushroom blend, coarsely chopped
2	garlic cloves, minced
2	tablespoons dry sherry
2	ounces Parmigiano-Reggiano cheese, divided
1/4	cup heavy whipping cream
1	teaspoon finely chopped fresh sage
1/2	teaspoon cracked black pepper
1	teaspoon truffle oil
	Sage sprigs (optional)

1. Rinse porcini thoroughly. Combine porcini and 2/3 cup boiling water in a bowl; cover and let stand 30 minutes. Drain in a sieve over a bowl, reserving 1/4 cup soaking liquid. Chop porcini.

2. Cook pasta with 1 tablespoon salt in boiling water 10 minutes or until al dente; drain in a colander over a bowl, reserving 1/4 cup cooking liquid.

3. Melt butter in a large skillet over medium-high heat. Add shallots, mushroom blend, and garlic; sauté 5 minutes, stirring frequently. Stir in porcini, sherry, and 1/2 teaspoon salt; cook 1 minute or until liquid evaporates.

4. Finely grate 1 ounce cheese; crumble remaining cheese. Reduce heat to medium. Stir in pasta, 1/4 cup reserved cooking liquid, 1/4 cup reserved porcini soaking liquid, remaining 1/4 teaspoon salt, 1/4 cup grated cheese, cream, chopped sage, and pepper; toss well to combine. Drizzle with oil; toss. Place about 1 1/4 cups pasta mixture on each of 4 plates; top each serving with about 1 tablespoon crumbled cheese. Garnish with sage sprigs, if desired. **Yield: 4 servings.**

CALORIES 393; FAT 14.2g (sat 7.9g, mono 4.3g, poly 0.9g); PROTEIN 15.8g; CARB 49.3g; FIBER 3.4g; CHOL 38mg; IRON 3.1mg; SODIUM 733mg; CALC 201mg

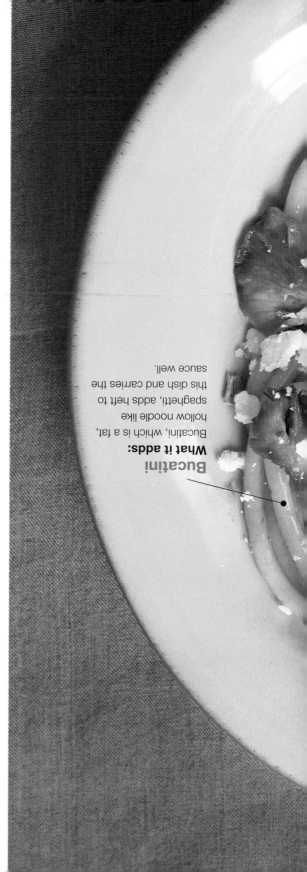

Bucatini
What it adds:

Bucatini, which is a fat, hollow noodle like spaghetti, adds heft to this dish and carries the sauce well.

Curried Vegetable Samosas with Cilantro-Mint Chutney

Chutney:
- ½ cup fresh cilantro leaves
- ½ cup fresh mint leaves
- ¼ cup chopped red onion
- 2 tablespoons fresh lemon juice
- 1 tablespoon water
- ¼ teaspoon kosher salt
- ⅛ teaspoon sugar
- 1 serrano chile, coarsely chopped
- 1 (½-inch) piece peeled fresh ginger

Samosas:
- 1¼ cups mashed cooked peeled baking potatoes
- ¼ cup cooked yellow lentils
- 1 tablespoon minced fresh mint
- 1 teaspoon Madras curry powder
- 1 teaspoon butter, softened
- ¼ teaspoon kosher salt
- ¼ teaspoon ground cumin
- ½ cup frozen petite green peas, thawed
- 10 egg roll wrappers
- 1 large egg, lightly beaten
- Cooking spray

1. To prepare chutney, combine first 9 ingredients in a blender; process until smooth. Set aside.

2. To prepare samosas, combine potatoes, lentils, mint, curry powder, 1 teaspoon butter, ¼ teaspoon salt, and cumin. Gently fold in peas.

3. Working with 1 egg roll wrapper at a time (cover remaining wrappers to prevent drying), cut down middle to form 2 long rectangles. Moisten edges of wrapper with egg. Spoon 1 tablespoon potato mixture near bottom edge of wrapper. Fold up from 1 corner to the opposite outer edge of the wrapper, making a triangle. Fold over to opposite side as if folding up a flag. Repeat fold to opposite side to form a triangle. Repeat with remaining wrappers and filling.

4. Heat a large cast-iron skillet over medium-high heat. Coat pan with cooking spray. Lightly coat samosas with cooking spray. Add samosas to pan, and cook 1 minute on each side. Drain on paper towels. Serve with chutney. **Yield: 4 servings (serving size: 5 samosas and about 1 tablespoon chutney).**

CALORIES 288; FAT 2.6g (sat 0.9g, mono 0.9g, poly 0.2g); PROTEIN 11g; CARB 58.3g; FIBER 5.4g; CHOL 29mg; IRON 4.6mg; SODIUM 574mg; CALC 43mg

kitchen how-to: shape samosas

These small, crisp, flaky pastries are truly international. Their origins are in Asia, but you can also find them in Indian, Middle Eastern, and African cuisines. They're usually made with a savory filling and served with chutney, marmalade, or sauce.

1. Working with 1 egg roll wrapper at a time (cover the remaining wrappers to prevent them from drying), cut down the middle to form 2 long rectangles. Moisten the edges of the wrapper with egg. Spoon the filling near the bottom edge of the wrapper. Fold up the wrapper from 1 corner

2. Fold over the wrapper to the opposite side again, as if you were folding a flag.

3. Repeat folding the wrapper to the opposite side to form a triangle.

way to cook vegetarian

eggs & dairy

eggs & dairy

The culinary range of eggs, milk, and cheese extends beyond breakfast. These foods are an inexpensive and flavorful source of nutrients, particularly protein, which makes them a valuable part of vegetarian meals—for breakfast, lunch, *and* dinner.

Eggs

Eggs are economical and might just be the world's most versatile food. Their neutral taste makes them a good vehicle for an array of flavors, and because they coagulate when they're cooked, they perform functions that no other ingredient can—they bind foods and provide structure. Eggs also fit conveniently into a healthy diet. For 72 calories and 1.6 grams of saturated fat, one egg offers 6.3 grams of protein and a bevy of beneficial nutrients, such as vitamin A, which promotes good vision and skin health; zinc, which aids in metabolism and immunity; lutein, which supports eye health; and vitamin B_{12}, which supports red blood cell production, growth and development in children, and maintenance of the nervous system. B_{12} is found primarily in meats, eggs, and dairy products, so it's important that vegetarians are vigilant about incorporating eggs and dairy into their diet.

kitchen how-to:
scramble eggs

Whisk eggs (along with butter, if you'd like) in a bowl. Pour the whisked eggs into a skillet, and cook over medium-high heat. Stir the eggs constantly, and cook about 3 minutes or until the eggs start to thicken slightly. Remove the pan from the heat, and continue stirring about 30 seconds; return the pan to the heat. Keep an eye on the heat—if the pan becomes too hot and the eggs start to seize, remove the pan from the heat, stirring constantly to fold the cooked eggs back into the uncooked ones. Continue cooking briefly and removing the pan from the heat, stirring constantly, until the eggs are almost set but still appear moist. Sprinkle the eggs with salt, pepper, and any other seasonings you'd like.

kitchen how-to:
make an omelet

Use a mix of seasonal ingredients, sautéed vegetables, or your favorite mushrooms to fill this classic French-style omelet. If the pan becomes too hot and the eggs begin to set too quickly, simply lift the pan off the heat to slow the cooking as you stir.

1. Melt butter in a hot skillet over medium-high heat, and pour the whisked eggs into the pan. Stir briskly with a heatproof spatula for about 10 seconds or until egg starts to thicken. Quickly pull the egg that sets at the sides of the pan to the center with the spatula, tipping the pan to allow the uncooked egg in the center to run out to the sides. Continue this procedure for 10 to 15 seconds or until almost no runny egg remains.

2. Remove the pan from the heat, and arrange the filling over the omelet in the pan. Run the spatula around the edges and under the omelet to loosen it from the pan.

3. To fold the omelet, hold the pan handle with one hand and tip the pan away from you. Fold the top edge of the omelet over with a fork, or give the handle a sharp tap with your other hand so the top edge flips over. Slide the omelet from the pan onto a plate, rolling it as it slides, so it lands folded in three with the seam underneath. Tuck in the sides of the omelet to neaten it.

Poached Eggs with Buttery Multigrain Toast

4 cups water
1 tablespoon white vinegar
4 large eggs
2 tablespoons butter, softened
4 (1½-ounce) slices multigrain bread
2 cups baby arugula
¼ teaspoon salt
¼ teaspoon freshly ground black pepper

1. Preheat broiler.
2. Combine 4 cups water and vinegar in a 12-inch skillet, and bring to a low boil. Break eggs, one at a time, into a bubbling area so the bubbles spin the egg and set the white around the yolks. Reduce heat, and poach 3 minutes or until desired degree of doneness. To test for doneness, lift eggs with a slotted spoon and press with your fingertip: The white should be set with the yolk still soft. Transfer eggs to a bowl of warm water. Trim strings from edges of each egg with kitchen shears, if desired.
3. Spread 1½ teaspoons butter over each bread slice. Place bread slices in a single layer on a heavy baking sheet; broil 3 minutes or until golden. Place 1 toasted bread slice on each of 4 plates; top each serving with ½ cup arugula and 1 egg. Sprinkle evenly with salt and pepper, and serve immediately. **Yield: 4 servings.**

CALORIES 231; FAT 12.3g (sat 5.5g, mono 4g, poly 1.3g); PROTEIN 10.9g; CARB 20.6g; FIBER 2.9g; CHOL 227mg; IRON 2.6mg; SODIUM 468mg; CALC 83mg

kitchen how-to:
poach eggs

Eggs can be poached ahead of time and stored in cold water in the refrigerator, but if so, be sure to undercook them slightly. Warm them in hot water before serving.

1. In a 12-inch skillet, bring a 2-inch layer of water (about 4 cups) to a low boil with 1 tablespoon of vinegar. The vinegar in the poaching water helps the egg whites set quickly. Break an egg into a bubbling area so the bubbles spin the egg and set the white around the yolks. Add the remaining eggs, and then turn down the heat, and poach the eggs so they scarcely bubble for 3 minutes or until the desired degree of doneness.
2. To test for doneness, carefully lift each egg with a slotted spoon and press it with your fingertips—the white should be set with the yolk still soft. Transfer the eggs to a plate, season, and serve. If you need to keep the eggs warm while you finish the rest of your meal, transfer the cooked eggs to a bowl of warm water until you're ready to serve them.

Baked Eggs en Cocotte with Onions

Keep an eye on the eggs as they cook, bearing in mind that cook times vary depending on the thickness of the ramekins and your personal preference for the texture of the eggs.

Cooking spray
4 (1-ounce) slices French-style country bread, cut into ½-inch cubes
1⅓ cups thinly sliced onion
½ teaspoon salt, divided
¼ teaspoon ground white pepper, divided
2 tablespoons water
6 large eggs
¼ cup half-and-half
Fresh flat-leaf parsley sprigs

1. Preheat oven to 350°.
2. Lightly coat 6 (8-ounce) ramekins with cooking spray. Spread bread cubes in an even layer on a baking sheet, and lightly coat with cooking spray. Bake at 350° for 10 minutes or until bread is crisp and lightly browned, stirring after 5 minutes.

3. Heat a small skillet over medium heat. Coat pan with cooking spray. Add onion, ¼ teaspoon salt, and ⅛ teaspoon pepper to pan; cook 10 minutes or until onion is tender. Increase heat to medium-high. Stir in 2 tablespoons water, and cook 5 minutes or until golden brown, stirring frequently. Evenly divide onion among prepared ramekins; top with croutons. Sprinkle remaining ¼ teaspoon salt and remaining ⅛ teaspoon pepper evenly over croutons.
4. Carefully break 1 egg into each ramekin on top of croutons; drizzle 2 teaspoons half-and-half over each egg. Arrange ramekins in a roasting pan lined with a dish towel (to anchor them in the pan). Pour boiling water halfway up sides of ramekins to make a water bath. Bake at 350° for 15 minutes or until whites are almost set. They should be slightly underdone as they will continue cooking in the hot dishes when you take them from the oven. Garnish with flat-leaf parsley sprigs, if desired. **Yield: 6 servings (serving size: 1 ramekin).**

CALORIES 163; FAT 6.7g (sat 2.3g, mono 1.9g, poly 0.7g); PROTEIN 8.9g; CARB 16.9g; FIBER 1.7g; CHOL 215mg; IRON 1.6mg; SODIUM 393mg; CALC 64mg

kitchen how-to:
tell if eggs are fresh

Fresh eggs taste and perform differently from older ones. The difference will be most noticeable in preparations that feature eggs prominently, such as baked or poached eggs or a plain omelet. In custards and other dishes where eggs play a background role, fresh eggs are not as critical. To gauge freshness, break an egg onto a plate. When the egg is fresh, the yolk will sit high with the white clinging closely around it and looking cloudy (as with the egg on the right). With an older egg, the white will be clear and watery, running all over the plate (pictured on the left). Don't keep whole eggs in the shell at home more than three weeks after you buy them.

Frittata with Spinach, Potatoes, and Leeks

Make the leek mixture, and cook the potatoes a day ahead. Or use store-bought diced cooked potatoes (such as Simply Potatoes), whisk the eggs, combine everything, and bake the frittata in the morning.

1 teaspoon butter
2 cups thinly sliced leek (about 2 large)
1 (10-ounce) package fresh spinach
⅓ cup fat-free milk
2 tablespoons finely chopped fresh basil
½ teaspoon salt
¼ teaspoon black pepper
4 large eggs
4 large egg whites
2 cups cooked, peeled, cubed red potato (about ¾ pound)
Cooking spray
1½ tablespoons dry breadcrumbs
½ cup (2 ounces) shredded provolone cheese

1. Preheat oven to 350°.
2. Melt butter in a skillet over medium heat. Add leek; sauté 4 minutes. Add spinach in two batches; sauté 2 minutes or until spinach wilts. Place mixture in a colander, pressing until barely moist.
3. Combine milk and next 5 ingredients in a bowl; stir well with a whisk. Add leek mixture and potato. Pour into a 10-inch round ceramic baking dish or pie plate coated with cooking spray. Sprinkle with breadcrumbs, and top with cheese. Bake at 350° for 25 minutes or until center is set.
4. Preheat broiler.
5. Broil frittata 4 minutes or until golden brown. Cut into wedges. **Yield: 6 servings (serving size: 1 wedge).**

CALORIES 185; FAT 7.1g (sat 3g, mono 1.5g, poly 0.6g); PROTEIN 12.5g; CARB 18.9g; FIBER 2.8g; CHOL 150mg; IRON 3mg; SODIUM 429mg; CALC 176mg

kitchen how-to:
make a frittata

Frittatas are easy and adaptable. You can add any vegetables you like, but just be sure to cook them before adding them to the egg mixture since the time in the oven really only cooks the egg. Plus, by sautéing or caramelizing the vegetables, you'll add a nice depth of flavor to the frittata. See page 133 for another method for cooking a frittata that uses an ovenproof skillet.

1. Sauté or caramelize the vegetables that will be used for the filling.
2. Depending on the type of filling ingredients you choose, you might need to drain them so they don't add excess water to the frittata. Place the filling ingredients in a colander, and press them until they're barely moist.
3. Combine the eggs and seasonings, stirring well with a whisk. Add the cooked filling ingredients to the egg mixture.
4. Pour the egg mixture into a 10-inch ceramic baking dish or pie plate coated with cooking spray.
5. Sprinkle with breadcrumbs or cheese or both, and bake at 350° for 25 minutes or until the center is set.
6. Broil the frittata for 4 minutes or until it's golden brown. Cut it into wedges, and serve.

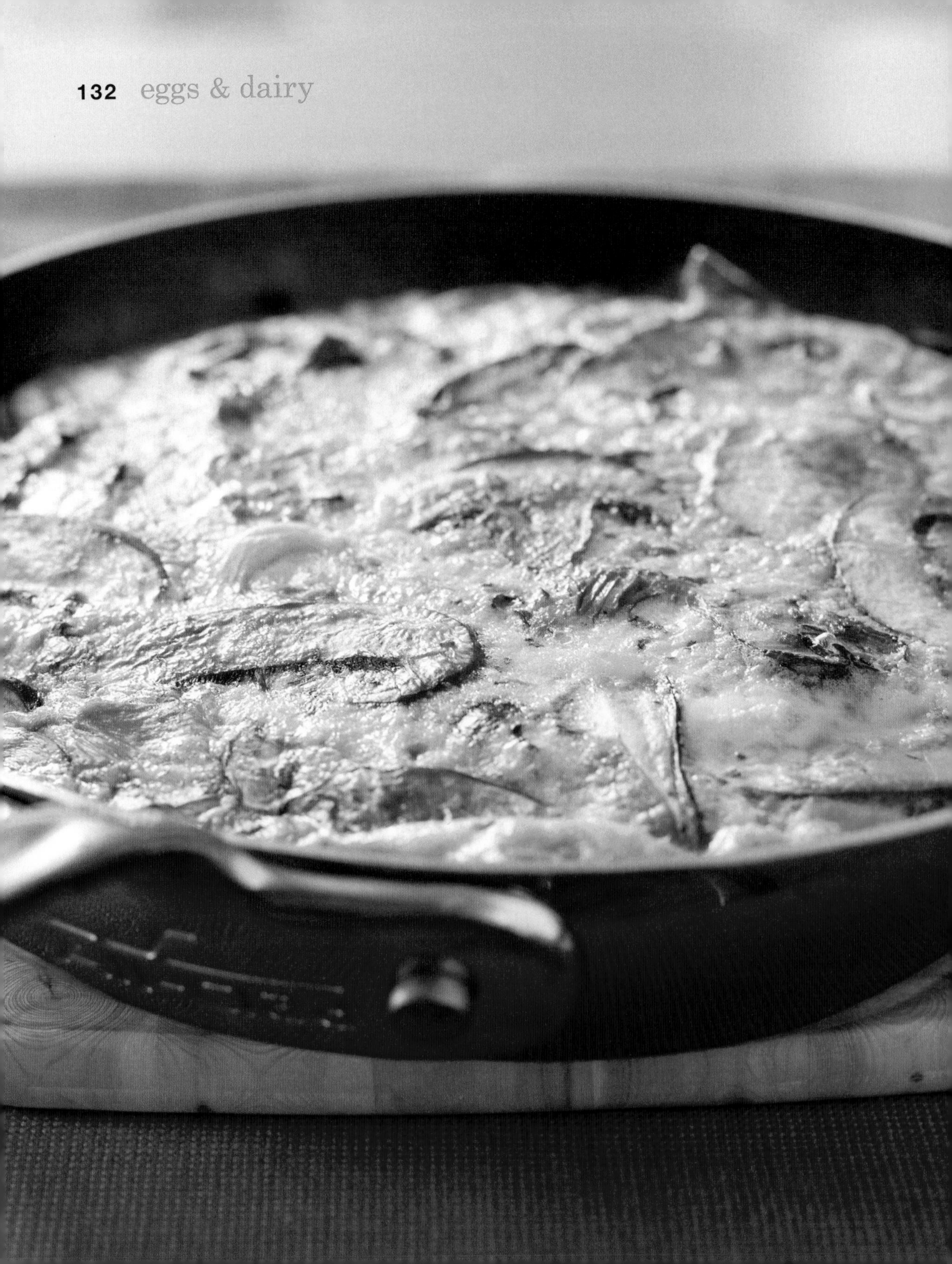

Brie and Egg Strata

You can substitute a French baguette or sourdough loaf for the ciabatta, if you'd like.

- 2 teaspoons olive oil
- 2 cups chopped onion
- 1½ cups diced unpeeled Yukon gold potato (1 large)
- 1 cup chopped red bell pepper
- 1 cup halved grape tomatoes
- 1 teaspoon salt, divided
- ¾ pound ciabatta, cut into 1-inch cubes, toasted
- Cooking spray
- 4 ounces Brie cheese, rind removed and chopped
- 1 cup egg substitute
- 2 large eggs
- 1 teaspoon herbes de Provence
- ¼ teaspoon freshly ground black pepper
- 3 cups 1% low-fat milk
- 2 tablespoons chopped fresh parsley

1. Heat oil in a large nonstick skillet over medium-high heat. Add onion, potato, and bell pepper; sauté 4 minutes or until tender. Stir in tomatoes; sauté 2 minutes. Stir in ½ teaspoon salt. Combine onion mixture and bread.

2. Place half of bread mixture into a 13 x 9–inch baking dish coated with cooking spray. Sprinkle with half of Brie. Top with remaining bread mixture and remaining Brie. Place egg substitute and eggs in a medium bowl. Add remaining ½ teaspoon salt, herbes de Provence, and pepper. Add milk, stirring with a whisk until well blended. Pour egg mixture over bread mixture. Let stand 30 minutes.

3. Preheat oven to 350°.

4. Bake at 350° for 50 minutes or until set. Sprinkle with parsley. Serve immediately. **Yield: 12 servings (serving size: 1 piece).**

CALORIES 205; FAT 6.9g (sat 2.7g, mono 3g, poly 0.8g); PROTEIN 10.8g; CARB 26.1g; FIBER 1.7g; CHOL 47mg; IRON 2mg; SODIUM 534mg; CALC 120mg

Potato and Greens Torta

A potato ricer gives this torta the most desirable texture.

1½ pounds small Yukon gold potatoes
3½ teaspoons fine sea salt, divided
 1 tablespoon extra-virgin olive oil
 3 garlic cloves, minced
 4 cups torn romaine lettuce
 2 cups packed fresh spinach leaves
 2 cups packed arugula leaves
 ½ cup 2% reduced-fat milk
 ½ cup (2 ounces) shredded fontina cheese
 2 large eggs, lightly beaten
Cooking spray
 3 tablespoons dry breadcrumbs
 ¼ cup (1 ounce) grated fresh pecorino Romano
   cheese

1. Preheat oven to 375°.
2. Place potatoes and 1 tablespoon salt in a large saucepan; cover with water. Bring to a boil. Reduce heat; simmer 15 minutes or until tender. Drain; cool slightly. Peel potatoes; discard peels. Press cooked potatoes through a ricer into a large bowl.
3. Heat oil in a large nonstick skillet over medium heat. Add garlic; cook 2 minutes, stirring frequently. Stir in romaine, spinach, and arugula; cook 1 minute or until greens wilt, tossing frequently. Remove greens from pan; finely chop.
4. Add greens, milk, fontina, eggs, and remaining ½ teaspoon salt to potatoes; stir well to combine. Coat a 9-inch pie plate with cooking spray; dust with bread-crumbs. Add potato mixture to prepared dish. Bake at 375° for 25 minutes. Remove from oven; sprinkle with pecorino. Let stand 10 minutes before serving. **Yield: 6 servings (serving size: 1 wedge).**

CALORIES 214; FAT 9.1g (sat 3.8g, mono 3.6g, poly 0.9g); PROTEIN 10.3g; CARB 24.2g; FIBER 3.2g; CHOL 88mg; IRON 2.1mg; SODIUM 520mg; CALC 189mg

kitchen how-to:
rice potatoes

Place the potatoes in a large saucepan, and cover them with water. Bring to a boil; reduce heat, and simmer 15 minutes or until tender. Drain the potatoes, and cool slightly. Peel the potatoes, and discard the peels. Press the cooked potatoes through a ricer into a large bowl. Ricers are inexpensive (as little as $10) and produce the creamiest mashed potatoes; if you don't have one, you can always use a handheld potato masher.

Garden Vegetable Crustless Quiche

1½   cups egg substitute
  3   large eggs
1½   cups (6 ounces) shredded reduced-fat extrasharp cheddar cheese, divided
1½   cups (6 ounces) shredded reduced-fat Monterey Jack cheese, divided
  ½   cup 1% low-fat milk
2.25   ounces all-purpose flour (about ½ cup)
  1   teaspoon baking powder
  ½   teaspoon salt
  1   (16-ounce) carton fat-free cottage cheese
Cooking spray
  4   cups sliced zucchini (about 4)
  2   cups diced potato with onion (such as Simply Potatoes)
  1   cup finely chopped green bell pepper (about 1)
  1   (8-ounce) package presliced mushrooms
  ½   cup chopped fresh parsley
  2   tomatoes, thinly sliced

1. Preheat oven to 400°.
2. Beat egg substitute and eggs in a large bowl until fluffy. Add ¾ cup cheddar cheese, ¾ cup Jack cheese, milk, and next 4 ingredients.
3. Heat a large nonstick skillet over medium-high heat; coat pan with cooking spray. Add zucchini and next 3 ingredients; sauté 5 minutes or until tender. Add the zucchini mixture and parsley to egg mixture. Pour mixture into a 3-quart casserole dish coated with cooking spray. Top with remaining ¾ cup cheddar cheese and ¾ cup Jack cheese. Arrange tomato slices over cheese. Bake at 400° for 15 minutes. Reduce oven temperature to 350° (do not remove dish from oven), and bake 35 minutes or until lightly browned and set.
Yield: 10 servings.

CALORIES 230; FAT 7.7g (sat 4.6g, mono 1.3g, poly 0.3g); PROTEIN 23g; CARB 18.1g; FIBER 1.9g; CHOL 84mg; IRON 2.1mg; SODIUM 716mg; CALC 382mg

1% Milk
What it adds: Some quiches use butter as the liquid, but using 1% milk yields a healthier quiche with less saturated fat.

Fat-Free Cottage Cheese
What it adds: The cottage cheese gives the quiche body and creaminess.

Cheddar and Monterey Jack Cheeses
What they add: The Jack has good melting properties to create a creamy texture, while the reduced-fat extrasharp cheddar exerts a stronger flavor.

Mushroom and Roasted Pepper Tarts

You can prepare these tarts up to two days ahead, chill them, and reheat them just before serving.

Chive Piecrust:
  5 ounces all-purpose flour (about 1¼ cups)
  ¼ teaspoon salt
  ¼ teaspoon baking powder
  2 tablespoons minced fresh chives
  ¼ cup vegetable shortening
  4 teaspoons unsalted butter, melted
  ¼ cup boiling water
  Cooking spray
  1 tablespoon Dijon mustard

Filling:
  1 cup boiling water
  ½ cup dried porcini mushrooms (about ½ ounce)
  1 tablespoon canola oil
  2 tablespoons chopped shallots
  4 ounces cremini mushrooms, thinly sliced
  3½ ounces shiitake mushroom caps, thinly sliced
  1 garlic clove, minced
  2 tablespoons Madeira wine
  1 teaspoon chopped fresh thyme
  1 tablespoon chopped fresh flat-leaf parsley
  1 teaspoon fresh lemon juice
  1 teaspoon freshly ground black pepper
  ¾ teaspoon kosher salt
  3 tablespoons grated Parmigiano-Reggiano cheese, divided
  ½ cup 2% reduced-fat evaporated milk
  2 tablespoons half-and-half
  1 large egg
  1 large egg white
  ⅓ cup chopped bottled roasted red bell peppers
  2 tablespoons finely chopped fresh chives

1. To make piecrust, weigh or lightly spoon flour into dry measuring cups; level with a knife. Combine flour and next 3 ingredients in a bowl; cut in shortening with a pastry blender until mixture resembles coarse meal.

2. Make a well in center of flour mixture. Combine butter and boiling water. Pour butter mixture into center of well. Gently draw flour mixture into butter mixture until moist clumps form. Press dough into a 4-inch circle. Cover, and chill 30 minutes.

3. Preheat oven to 400°.

4. Divide chive piecrust dough into 5 equal portions. Place each portion between two sheets of plastic wrap; roll into a 6-inch circle. Remove top sheet of plastic wrap. Place each dough circle, plastic wrap side up, into a 4-inch round tart pan coated with cooking spray. Remove remaining plastic wrap. Press dough into bottom and up sides of pan; fold excess crust back in, and press. Pierce bottom and sides of dough lightly with a fork; freeze 10 minutes. Line bottoms of dough with foil; top with pie weights or dried beans. Bake at 400° for 25 minutes or until lightly browned. Cool on a wire rack 15 minutes; remove weights and foil. Brush crusts with mustard.

5. Reduce oven temperature to 375°.

6. To make filling, combine 1 cup boiling water and porcini mushrooms in a bowl; cover and let stand 20 minutes. Strain mixture through a sieve over a bowl, reserving mushrooms and ¼ cup liquid. Finely chop mushrooms.

7. Heat oil in a large skillet over medium heat. Add shallots; cook 1 minute. Add cremini and shiitake mushrooms; cook 8 minutes, stirring occasionally. Add garlic; cook 1 minute, stirring occasionally. Stir in porcini mushrooms, wine, and thyme; cook 1 minute. Add reserved ¼ cup soaking liquid, scraping pan to loosen browned bits. Reduce heat; cook 3 minutes. Stir in parsley, juice, pepper, and salt.

8. Divide mushroom mixture evenly among prepared crusts. Combine 2 tablespoons cheese and next 4 ingredients, stirring with a whisk; divide evenly among tarts. Sprinkle evenly with bell peppers and remaining cheese. Place tarts on a baking sheet. Bake at 375° for 35 minutes or until set. Cool on a wire rack 10 minutes. Sprinkle with chives. **Yield: 5 servings (serving size: 1 tart).**

CALORIES 332; FAT 17.2g (sat 6.3g, mono 7.4g, poly 2.1g); PROTEIN 10.6g; CARB 31.1g; FIBER 2.5g; CHOL 57mg; IRON 2.9mg; SODIUM 708mg; CALC 165mg

kitchen how-to: make flaky, light piecrust

Vegetable shortening gives the piecrust a flaky texture. Read the nutrition labels, and buy a brand that doesn't contain trans fat. A small bit of butter adds flavor while keeping the saturated fat in check.

1. Weigh or carefully measure the flour. If you use too much flour, you'll have a dense, dry, and floury-tasting crust. Invest in an inexpensive scale, which will help ensure success every time you bake.

2. After weighing the flour, combine it with the other dry ingredients, such as salt and baking powder, stirring well. Separately combine the wet ingredients. Using a flexible spatula, slowly incorporate the dry ingredients into the wet, and stir just until the dough is evenly moistened throughout.

3. The dough will be clumpy at this point, just as it should be. Don't knead it, but simply gather it up, gently press into a disk, wrap, and let it rest in the refrigerator so the glutens will relax.

4. This is a delicate dough, so it's easiest to roll it out to an even thickness between sheets of plastic wrap. This prevents the dough from sticking to the surface and tearing as you go.

gratins

The term "gratin" is French and actually refers to the browned bits on top of this rich dish. The golden deliciousness is easy to achieve.

Potato Gratin

1 garlic clove, peeled and halved
1 tablespoon unsalted butter, softened
2½ cups whole milk
2 tablespoons minced shallots
¼ teaspoon kosher salt
¼ teaspoon black pepper
Dash of grated whole nutmeg
2 pounds Yukon gold potatoes, peeled and cut into ⅛-inch-thick slices
½ cup (2 ounces) shredded Gruyère cheese
¼ cup (1 ounce) grated fresh Parmigiano-Reggiano cheese

1. Preheat oven to 375°.
2. Rub a broiler-safe 11 x 7–inch baking dish with garlic; discard garlic. Coat dish with butter. Combine milk and next 5 ingredients in a skillet; bring to a simmer. Cook 8 minutes or until potatoes are almost tender. Spoon potato mixture into prepared baking dish. Sprinkle with cheeses. Bake at 375° for 35 minutes.
3. Preheat broiler. Broil 3 minutes or until golden. Let stand 10 minutes.
Yield: 8 servings (serving size: about ½ cup).

CALORIES 198; FAT 7.2G (SAT 4.3G, MONO 2G, POLY 0.4G); PROTEIN 8.7G; CARB 24.1G; FIBER 1.4G; CHOL 22MG; IRON 1.1MG; SODIUM 311MG; CALC 204MG

kitchen how-to: make great gratins

All gratins have one thing in common: a browned top. As a result, the varieties and interpretations are countless. Just pick your vegetable (or a couple of vegetables); add a flavorful liquid or sauce; sprinkle the top with breadcrumbs, cheese, or combination of the two; and bake. Although gratins are often vegetable-based, you can cook pasta or other starches au gratin for a change of pace—simply follow these steps, but just use a starch instead of vegetables, or combine them. You can also add cooked beans or tofu before baking to amp up the protein.

1. You can choose the size and shape of your vegetables as long as they're all the same size so they'll cook evenly. Thin or thick slices work just as well as small- to medium-sized cubes. Of course, thicker, larger pieces will take a little more time to cook.

2. Once you cut the vegetables, partially cook them in milk, broth, or water until they're almost tender. This cuts down on the amount of time the dish has to bake once assembled. If you want to get a jump start on the recipe, you can prepare and assemble the gratin ahead of time, but leave off the topping.

3. Spoon the vegetable (or pasta) mixture into a baking dish coated with cooking spray or butter, and top it with breadcrumbs, cheese, or a combination of the two. The breadcrumbs will brown easily and become crisp if they're tossed with a bit of butter. Cheese browns well, too. You can also add finely chopped nuts to the topping. Cook until browned and bubbly. Broil it for the last few minutes to ensure a nice browned top.

cheese-based dishes

Simply put: Cheese is delicious, and its protein and calcium content make it a great addition to vegetarian meals.

Cheese Pie with Peppers

Cooking spray
1½ cups chopped green bell pepper
1 tablespoon finely chopped seeded jalapeño pepper (about 1 medium)
2.25 ounces semolina or pasta flour (about ½ cup)
1½ cups fat-free milk, divided
1 cup plain fat-free yogurt
1 cup (4 ounces) crumbled feta cheese
1 cup (4 ounces) shredded reduced-fat extrasharp cheddar cheese
¼ cup (1 ounce) crumbled blue cheese
½ teaspoon salt
¼ teaspoon freshly ground black pepper
2 large egg whites
8 (18 x 14–inch) sheets frozen phyllo dough, thawed

1. Preheat oven to 400°.
2. Heat a large nonstick skillet over medium-high heat; coat pan with cooking spray. Add bell pepper and jalapeño; sauté 5 minutes. Stir in flour; remove from heat. Set aside 2 tablespoons milk. Gradually add remaining milk to pan, stirring well with a whisk. Stir in yogurt; bring to a boil. Remove from heat; stir 2 minutes or until thick. Cool 5 minutes. Stir in cheeses, salt, black pepper, and egg whites.
3. Working with 1 phyllo sheet at a time (cover remaining dough to keep from drying), place 2 phyllo sheets in a 13 x 9–inch baking pan coated with cooking spray; gently press sheets into bottom and sides of pan, allowing ends to extend over edges of pan. Coat top sheet with cooking spray. Fold 1 phyllo sheet in half crosswise; place on sheets in bottom of pan, and coat with cooking spray. Top with 1 phyllo sheet, gently pressing sheet into bottom and sides of pan; coat with cooking spray. Spread cheese mixture evenly over top of phyllo. Fold 1 phyllo sheet in half crosswise; gently press on cheese mixture in pan, and coat with cooking spray. Top with remaining 3 phyllo sheets, coating each sheet with cooking spray. Cut ends of sheets extending over pan. Fold edges of phyllo to form a rim; flatten rim with fork. Cut 4 slits in the top of the phyllo with a sharp knife; brush with reserved 2 tablespoons milk. Bake at 400° for 22 minutes. Reduce oven temperature to 375° (do not remove pie from oven); bake 20 minutes or until browned. Remove from oven; let stand 15 minutes.
Yield: 8 servings (serving size: 1 piece).

CALORIES 243; FAT 8.7g (sat 5.2g, mono 1.7g, poly 0.4g); PROTEIN 13.3g; CARB 27.6g; FIBER 1.4g; CHOL 27mg; IRON 1.5mg; SODIUM 641mg; CALC 292mg

kitchen how-to:
assemble cheese pie with peppers

In addition to feta, this Greek specialty traditionally uses kopanisti and graviera cheeses; this version uses more readily available cheddar and blue cheeses.

1. Spread the cheese mixture evenly over the top of the phyllo. Then fold 1 phyllo sheet in half crosswise; gently press the phyllo sheet onto the cheese mixture in the pan, and coat with cooking spray. Top with the remaining 3 phyllo sheets, coating each sheet with cooking spray. The phyllo that hangs over the rim tends to dry out, so trim it off.
2. Fold the edges of the phyllo to form a rim; flatten the rim with a fork. Cut 4 slits in the top of the phyllo with a sharp knife; brush the top with the reserved 2 tablespoons milk, and bake the pie according to the recipe directions.

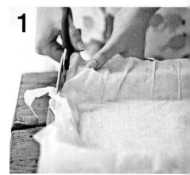

Spinach-Cheese Bake

You can assemble this casserole in less than 10 minutes by using preshredded cheeses. Pair this dish with a fresh berry salad and mini muffins for a lovely brunch.

1	tablespoon butter, melted
	Cooking spray
2	(6-ounce) packages fresh baby spinach
1¼	cups (5 ounces) shredded reduced-fat sharp cheddar cheese
¾	cup (3 ounces) shredded Monterey Jack cheese
5.75	ounces all-purpose flour (about 1⅓ cups)
1½	cups fat-free milk
1	cup egg substitute
1	teaspoon salt
1	teaspoon baking powder
2	teaspoons Dijon mustard
¼	teaspoon freshly ground black pepper
⅛	teaspoon ground nutmeg
⅛	teaspoon ground red pepper

1. Preheat oven to 350°.

2. Pour butter into the bottom of a 13 x 9–inch baking dish coated with cooking spray; tilt dish to coat. Place spinach evenly in bottom of dish; sprinkle evenly with cheeses.

3. Weigh or lightly spoon flour into dry measuring cups; level with a knife. Combine flour and remaining ingredients in a medium bowl; stir with a whisk until blended. Pour milk mixture over cheese. Bake at 350° for 40 minutes or until lightly browned. Cut into 12 wedges, and serve immediately. **Yield: 12 servings (serving size: 1 wedge).**

CALORIES 157; FAT 6g (sat 3.7G, mono 1.7g, poly 0.4g); PROTEIN 10.8g; CARB 15.1g; FIBER 1.6g; CHOL 18mg; IRON 2.6mg; SODIUM 494mg; CALC 263mg

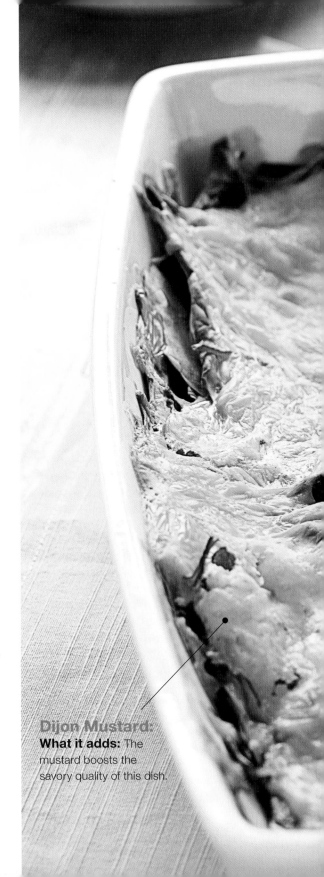

Dijon Mustard:
What it adds: The mustard boosts the savory quality of this dish.

Egg Substitute:
What it adds: By using egg substitute instead of whole eggs, we saved on calories and fat, which helps keep this hearty dish nutritionally in check.

Spinach:
What it adds: Spinach adds color, as well as fiber and iron, to this dish.

ricotta

Homemade ricotta cheese is easy to make, and after tasting the creamy results, you'll find it's well worth the effort.

Homemade Ricotta Cheese

You can store this cheese in the refrigerator for up to four days.

- 1 **gallon 2% reduced-fat milk**
- 5 **cups low-fat buttermilk**
- ½ **teaspoon fine sea salt**

1. Line a large colander or sieve with 5 layers of dampened cheesecloth, allowing cheesecloth to extend over outside edges of colander; place colander in a large bowl.
2. Combine milk and buttermilk in a large, heavy stockpot. Attach a candy thermometer to edge of pan so that thermometer extends at least 2 inches into milk mixture. Cook over medium-high heat until candy thermometer registers 170° (about 20 minutes), gently stirring occasionally. As soon as milk mixture reaches 170°, stop stirring (whey and curds will begin separating at this point). Continue to cook, without stirring, until thermometer registers 190°. (Be sure not to stir, or curds that have formed will break apart.) Immediately remove pan from heat. (Bottom of pan may be slightly scorched.)
3. Using a slotted spoon, gently spoon curds into cheesecloth-lined colander; discard whey, or reserve it for another use. Drain over bowl 5 minutes. Gather edges of cheesecloth together; tie securely. Hang cheesecloth bundle from kitchen faucet; drain 15 minutes or until whey stops dripping. Scrape ricotta into a bowl. Sprinkle with salt; toss gently with a fork to combine. Cool to room temperature. **Yield: About 3 cups (serving size: ¼ cup).**

CALORIES 115; FAT 6.1g (sat 3.8g, mono 1.8g, poly 0.2g); PROTEIN 11.5g; CARB 3.5g; FIBER 0g; CHOL 23mg; IRON 0mg; SODIUM 191mg; CALC 250mg

kitchen how-to:
make ricotta cheese

Buy a candy thermometer that can clamp onto the lip of the pot, which will allow you to obtain an accurate temperature reading as you heat the milk.

1. Combine the milk and buttermilk in a large, heavy stockpot. Immerse the tip of the candy thermometer 2 inches into the liquid to ensure an accurate reading once the curds rise to the top. Cook over medium-high heat until the candy thermometer registers 170° (about 20 minutes). As the milk mixture heats to 170°, be sure to stir gently and occasionally; if you stir too vigorously or too frequently (more than every few minutes), the curds may not separate as effectively from the whey. As soon as the milk mixture reaches 170°, stop stirring (whey and curds will begin separating at this point), or the cheese will become grainy and thin.

2. Continue to cook without stirring until the thermometer registers 190°. Be sure not to stir, or the curds that have formed will break apart. Immediately remove pan from heat. The bottom of the pan may be slightly scorched. Gently scoop out the curds with a slotted spoon, trying not to agitate them or break them apart. Discard whey, or reserve it for another use. Drain over a bowl for 5 minutes.

3. Gather edges of cheesecloth; tie into a bag. Be careful not to squeeze the bag or push on the curds.

4. Hang the cheesecloth bag from kitchen faucet to allow the whey to drain out. If your kitchen sink has a gooseneck faucet, it might be difficult to hang the cheesecloth bag on it. If so, lay a long wooden spoon across one corner of the sink, and hang the bag on the spoon handle. Drain 15 minutes or until the whey stops dropping.

5. Scrape the ricotta into a bowl. Sprinkle with salt, and toss gently with a fork to combine. Cool to room temperature.

Roasted Fennel and Ricotta Gratins with Tarragon

A sprinkling of fresh breadcrumbs gives each of these easy individual gratins a crispy top.

6¼   cups thinly sliced fennel bulb (about
     2 medium bulbs)
   Cooking spray
 ½   teaspoon salt, divided
 ¾   cup (6 ounces) Homemade Ricotta Cheese
     (page 148)
  1 (1½-ounce) slice hearty white bread (such as
     Pepperidge Farm)
  1 teaspoon minced fresh tarragon
 ¼   teaspoon freshly ground black pepper

1. Preheat oven to 450°.
2. Arrange fennel on a baking sheet coated with cooking spray, and sprinkle evenly with ¼ teaspoon salt. Bake at 450° for 40 minutes or until fennel is crisp-tender, stirring occasionally.
3. Reduce oven temperature to 375°.
4. Combine fennel, remaining ¼ teaspoon salt, and the Homemade Ricotta Cheese, tossing well. Divide mixture evenly among 6 (4-ounce) gratin dishes or ramekins coated with cooking spray.
5. Place bread in a food processor; pulse 10 times or until coarse crumbs measure ¾ cup. Combine breadcrumbs, tarragon, and pepper, tossing well. Sprinkle about 2 tablespoons breadcrumb mixture over each gratin dish. Bake at 375° for 20 minutes or until golden.
Yield: 6 servings (serving size: 1 gratin).

CALORIES 107; FAT 3.6g (sat 2g, mono 1g, poly 0.1g); PROTEIN 7.5g; CARB 12g; FIBER 3g; CHOL 11mg; IRON 0.9mg; SODIUM 380mg; CALC 177mg

Blueberry-Orange Parfaits

This snack comes together in a few minutes if you purchase the orange sections from the refrigerated part of the produce section. You can assemble the parfaits, except for the wheat germ, ahead, and refrigerate them, covered, for up to four hours; sprinkle the wheat germ over the top just before serving.

1½ tablespoons Demerara or turbinado sugar
½ teaspoon grated orange rind
2 (7-ounce) containers reduced-fat plain Greek-style yogurt
2 cups fresh blueberries
2 cups orange sections (about 2 large)
¼ cup wheat germ

1. Combine first 3 ingredients in a small bowl, stirring until blended. Spoon ¼ cup blueberries into each of 4 tall glasses. Spoon about 2½ tablespoons yogurt mixture over blueberries in each glass. Add ¼ cup orange to each serving. Repeat layers with remaining blueberries, yogurt mixture, and orange. Sprinkle 1 tablespoon wheat germ over each serving; serve immediately. **Yield: 4 servings (serving size: 1 parfait).**

CALORIES 186; FAT 3g (sat 1.6g, mono 0.1g, poly 0.5g); PROTEIN 11.8g; CARB 31.9g; FIBER 4.2g; CHOL 5mg; IRON 1mg; SODIUM 34mg; CALC 125mg

Vanilla Honey-Nut Smoothie

You can use any nut butter, either store-bought or homemade (see below and next page), to change up the flavor of this smoothie.

2 cups vanilla low-fat frozen yogurt
½ cup vanilla soy milk
½ cup fat-free milk
⅓ cup cubed soft silken tofu
1 tablespoon creamy peanut butter
1 tablespoon honey
1 tablespoon ground flaxseed (optional)

1. Combine first 6 ingredients in a blender; process until smooth. Sprinkle with flaxseed, if desired. **Yield: 3 servings (serving size: 1 cup).**

CALORIES 270; FAT 9g (sat 2.8g, mono 2.7g, poly 2g); PROTEIN 9.2g; CARB 41.5g; FIBER 0.6g; CHOL 14mg; IRON 1.8mg; SODIUM 117mg; CALC 250mg

kitchen how-to: make nut butters

Homemade nut butters taste much better but are more perishable than commercial varieties, so make them in small batches. You can store homemade butters covered in the refrigerator for up to a month. To make spreading easier, let the nut butter return to room temperature. As a general rule, there is a 2-to-1 ratio of nuts used to the nut butter yield (for example,

1 cup of nuts will make ½ cup nut butter). Place the nuts in a food processer, and process until they form a paste. (See All About Nut Butter on next page for specific processing times.) Some nut butters will be creamy; others a bit grainy. The higher the fat, the smoother the nut butter.

all about homemade nut butters

1. Almond: Slivered, toasted almonds take about 3½ minutes to form a butter, but roasted whole almonds have additional oil and will be ready in just 2½ minutes. This mild, sweet butter is adaptable in sweet and savory applications. Try it on a sandwich with apples and Brie or Gouda cheese.

2. Macadamia: Macadamias, which have a high fat content, grind into a butter in just 2 minutes, but it's too thin to immediately spread on bread. Chill this nut butter to thicken it.

3. Pecan: Pecans process into rich butter in about a minute. The loose paste spreads easily, but the skins give it a slightly bitter aftertaste, which makes it better suited for recipes than sandwiches.

4. Pistachio: This very dry, crumbly butter is best combined with something else, like softened cream cheese. It takes about 3½ to 4 minutes to grind into butter, and it tends to clump during processing.

5. Cashew: This smooth butter forms in about 2 minutes of processing. It's ideal for sandwiches. Try it with avocado and other vegetables in a pita, or substitute it for tahini when you make hummus.

6. Hazelnut: This grainy, thick butter with brown specks is fruity and naturally sweet. Processing it takes about 2½ minutes. Chopped nuts have few skins, so don't worry about removing them. If the nuts are whole, toast them in a 400° oven for 5 minutes or until they start to look shiny and the skins begin to loosen. Rub the nuts in a dishtowel to remove skins.

7. Peanut: Use plain roasted peanuts rather than dry-roasted, which are seasoned with paprika, garlic, and onion powder. This smooth nut butter has a distinctive fresh peanut flavor, and the nuts take about 2 minutes to process.

8. Walnut: Like pecan butter, this soft, oily butter is ready in about a minute. It, too, has a bitter aftertaste from the skins, making it good for recipes but not on sandwiches. Walnut halves are expensive, so look for pieces.

way to cook vegetarian

legumes & vegetables

learn how to

legumes & vegetables

The wide variety of legumes and vegetables that are available offers endless options for hearty and filling vegetarian meals.

Legumes

Legumes such as lentils, beans, and peas provide a healthy package of nutrients. They are high in protein and fiber, low in fat, and cholesterol free.

Lentils

Lentils are one of the oldest cultivated legumes, and their versatility easily takes them from dips to soups and salads—and cuisines from France to India and the Middle East. Lentils contain metabolism-boosting B vitamins as well as magnesium for bone health and iron for healthy red blood cells. Plus, a cup of cooked lentils provides 90 percent of the recommended daily allowance of folic acid, a nutrient particularly important for women of child-bearing age because it can guard against birth defects.

Lentils are sold both dried and canned. Dried varieties are more widely available and can be found in different sizes and colors, ranging from yellow and red-orange to green and brown, all of which can be purchased whole or split. Lentils have an advantage over other dried legumes—they are more convenient. Dried beans and peas need to be presoaked before cooking and often take more than an hour of simmering to become tender. But lentils are small and flat, which means that the cooking liquid doesn't have far to penetrate so they cook relatively quickly (usually 40 minutes or less) with no need for presoaking. For an even more convenient option, look for canned lentils in the organic section of some larger grocery stores.

brown lentils   red lentils   green lentils   black lentils

Beans

High in protein, beans are the centerpiece of many wonderful meatless dishes—think of kidney beans in chili, garbanzo beans in bean-based falafel, and black beans and rice. You can buy beans both dried and canned, and each has pros and cons. Dried varieties are less expensive than canned and often have superior taste and texture, but they require lengthy preparation, including time to soak and simmer. The good news is that most of the preparation is hands-off time; learn how to prepare dried beans on page 171. Canned beans are convenient, but they contain more sodium—ranging from about 350 to 630 milligrams per half cup compared to about 1 to 5 milligrams in the same amount of dried beans cooked without salt. One way to reduce the sodium content of canned beans is to rinse them; see page 180 for more information.

Peas

Peas are sold fresh, frozen, and canned, which makes them readily available year-round. Frozen peas offer a great option since they're frozen at the peak of freshness and retain their valuable nutrients. Canned peas are another convenient option, but that convenience comes with a higher sodium content than frozen or fresh ones; look for no-salt-added varieties to save yourself some sodium. When buying fresh peas, choose young, well-filled pods that are velvety soft to the touch. Peas that look as if they're about to explode are too mature and will taste tough and mealy when cooked. To prevent the sugar in the peas from converting to starch, store them in their pods, uncovered, in the refrigerator, and use them within two to three days of when you purchase them.

Vegetable Main Dishes

Although vegetables are often relegated to the side of a plate, they have the potential to be so much more. Vegetables are nutritional powerhouses—low in calories and brimming with a multitude of vitamins, minerals, antioxidants, and a host of other good-for-you compounds—plus they're full of flavor. We're partial to fresh, in-season vegetables since that's when they're at their best in terms of flavor, texture, and appearance. In this chapter we show you how to transform a traditional sidekick into the star of the plate.

lentils

At 25 percent protein, lentils have one of the highest protein levels of any vegetable. They're a widely adaptable, nutritious staple that serves as the basis of many comforting, satisfying dishes.

Turkish Carrots and Lentils (*Zeytinyagli Havuç*)

3	tablespoons extra-virgin olive oil
1½	cups thinly sliced onion
1	garlic clove, minced
1	tablespoon tomato paste
½	teaspoon ground Aleppo pepper
1	pound carrots, halved lengthwise and thinly sliced (about 3 cups)
¾	teaspoon sea salt, divided
3	cups water
1	cup uncooked dried green lentils
¼	teaspoon freshly ground black pepper
¼	cup Greek-style yogurt (such as Fage)

Fresh dill sprigs (optional)

1. Heat oil in a large saucepan over medium heat. Add onion; cook 9 minutes or until lightly browned, stirring occasionally. Add garlic; cook 1 minute. Stir in tomato paste and Aleppo pepper; cook 30 seconds. Stir in carrots and ¼ teaspoon salt; cook 1 minute. Remove from heat.

2. Combine 3 cups water and lentils in a large saucepan, and bring to a boil. Cover, reduce heat, and simmer 30 minutes. Uncover, increase heat to medium-high, and stir in onion mixture; cook 2 minutes or until liquid almost evaporates. Stir in remaining ½ teaspoon salt and freshly ground black pepper. Cover with a kitchen towel, and cool to room temperature. Serve with yogurt. Garnish with dill, if desired. **Yield: 4 servings (serving size: about 1 cup lentil mixture and 1 tablespoon yogurt).**

CALORIES 357; FAT 12.2g (sat 2.8g, mono 7.7g, poly 1.2g); PROTEIN 17.4g; CARB 48.6g; FIBER 10.6g; CHOL 3mg; IRON 5mg; SODIUM 549mg; CALC 64mg

kitchen how-to: cook lentils

Lentils cooks quickly and don't require soaking like other dried legumes do. They lend mild, nutty flavor that melds well with a wide variety of ingredients.

1. Combine the water and lentils in a large saucepan—3 cups of water for 1 cup of dried lentils is a good ratio.

2. Bring to a boil.

3. Cover, reduce the heat, and simmer 30 minutes.

4. Uncover, increase the heat to medium-high, and, if desired, stir in any cooked vegetables or seasonings you like; cook for 2 minutes or until the liquid almost evaporates.

5. Cover with a kitchen towel, and cool.

Red Lentil Dal with Charred Onions

Lentils are a great source of fiber. This dish provides 20 percent of your daily fiber goal. Serve the lentils over brown rice with a side of broccoli for a vegetarian meal.

- 1 tablespoon olive oil, divided
- 1 medium onion, cut into ¼-inch-thick slices
- 1 teaspoon mustard seeds
- ½ teaspoon coriander seeds
- ½ teaspoon cumin seeds
- 1 whole clove
- ¼ teaspoon ground cinnamon
- ⅛ teaspoon ground cardamom
- 1 dried hot red chile
- 1 tablespoon minced peeled fresh ginger
- 1 garlic clove, minced
- 4 cups organic vegetable broth (such as Swanson Certified Organic)
- 1 cup dried small red lentils
- 1 (14.5-ounce) can no-salt-added diced tomatoes, undrained
- ¼ cup chopped fresh cilantro
- 1 tablespoon fresh lime juice

1. Heat 1 teaspoon oil in a Dutch oven over medium-high heat. Add onion to pan; cook 2 minutes or until charred. Carefully turn over onion, and cook an additional 4 minutes or until blackened and charred. Remove from heat. Coarsely chop; set aside.

2. Combine mustard seeds, coriander seeds, cumin seeds, and clove in a small skillet over medium heat. Cook 1½ minutes or until fragrant, stirring frequently. Remove from heat. Combine mustard mixture, cinnamon, cardamom, and chile in spice or coffee grinder. Pulse until ground.

3. Heat remaining 2 teaspoons oil in a Dutch oven over medium-high heat. Add ginger and garlic to pan; sauté 1 minute. Stir in spices; sauté 1 minute. Add broth, lentils, and tomatoes to pan; bring to a boil. Cover, reduce heat, and simmer 30 minutes, stirring occasionally. Uncover; add onion, and cook 10 minutes. Stir in cilantro and juice. **Yield: 7 servings (serving size: 1 cup).**

CALORIES 149; FAT 2.8g (sat 0.3g, mono 1.6g, poly 0.3g); PROTEIN 8.4g; CARB 23.6g; FIBER 5.5g; CHOL 0mg; IRON 2.1mg; SODIUM 354mg; CALC 33mg

kitchen how-to:
make red lentil dal with charred onions

Traditional Indian dals can be made using lentils or beans. The texture of the dal depends on the water-to-dal ratio. The more water, the thinner the dal; less water produces a thicker dal. A good rule of thumb is 4 to 5 cups of water or liquid such as broth for every cup of dried lentils or beans.

1. Cook the onion in 1 teaspoon of olive oil in a Dutch oven over medium-high heat until the onion is charred. Remove the pan from the heat. Coarsely chop the onion, and set it aside.

2. Combine the mustard seeds, coriander seeds, cumin seeds, and clove in a small skillet over medium heat. Cook 1½ minutes or until fragrant, stirring frequently. Remove the pan from the heat. Toasting the spices gives them a deep, roasted flavor.

3. Combine the toasted spices, cinnamon, cardamom, and chile in a spice or coffee grinder, and pulse until they're ground.

4. Heat 2 teaspoons of oil in a Dutch oven over medium-high heat. Add the ginger and garlic, and sauté 1 minute. Stir in the spices, and sauté 1 minute.

5. Add the broth, lentils, and tomato to the pan; bring to a boil. Cover, reduce heat, and simmer 30 minutes, stirring occasionally.

6. Uncover; add the onion, and cook 10 minutes. Stir in the cilantro and juice.

Root Vegetable Tagine with Lentils

Spice Blend:

- ½ teaspoon salt
- ½ teaspoon ground cumin
- ½ teaspoon paprika
- ¼ teaspoon ground cinnamon
- ¼ teaspoon ground turmeric
- ¼ teaspoon curry powder
- ¼ teaspoon black pepper
- ⅛ teaspoon ground red pepper
- ⅛ teaspoon ground allspice

Tagine:

- 1 tablespoon olive oil
- 3 cups chopped green cabbage
- 2 cups (1-inch) cubed peeled sweet potato (about 12 ounces)
- 1 cup coarsely chopped onion
- 1 cup (1-inch-thick) slices parsnip
- 1 cup (1-inch-thick) slices carrot
- 1 cup (1-inch) cubed peeled turnip
- 1 cup dried lentils
- ½ cup chopped dried apricots
- 1 tablespoon minced peeled fresh ginger
- 2 teaspoons grated lemon rind
- 2 (14½-ounce) cans vegetable broth
- 1 (14.5-ounce) can diced tomatoes, undrained
- 1 tablespoon fresh lemon juice
- 6 cups hot cooked couscous

1. To prepare spice blend, combine first 9 ingredients.
2. To prepare tagine, heat oil in a Dutch oven over medium heat. Add cabbage and next 8 ingredients; cook 3 minutes, stirring frequently. Stir in spice blend; cook 1 minute, stirring constantly. Add rind, broth, and tomatoes; bring to a boil. Reduce heat; simmer, uncovered, 40 minutes or until lentils are tender. Stir in juice. Serve over couscous. **Yield: 8 servings (serving size: 1¼ cups tagine and ¾ cup couscous).**

CALORIES 343; FAT 2.7g (sat 0.3g, mono 1.3g, poly 0.4g); PROTEIN 13.4g; CARB 68.4g; FIBER 10.3g; CHOL 0mg; IRON 3.1mg; SODIUM 691mg; CALC 85mg

Sweet Potato
What it adds: Sweet potatoes are nutritional powerhouses. An excellent source of beta-carotene, they're also a good source of vitamin C, dietary fiber, and potassium.

Parsnip

What it adds: With a subtle, nutty flavor, parsnips offer nearly 7 grams of fiber and a dose of immunity aids including vitamin E, selenium, and zinc in every cup.

Turnip

What it adds: Each cup of this root vegetable provides more than 2 grams of fiber plus cancer-fighting compounds known as indoles.

beans & peas

Beans and peas are low in fat, free of cholesterol, and high in protein and fiber, which makes them an ideal base for meatless dishes.

White Beans with Roasted Red Pepper and Pesto

Pesto:

- 2 cups loosely packed basil leaves
- ½ cup (2 ounces) grated fresh Parmesan cheese
- 2 tablespoons pine nuts, toasted
- 2 tablespoons water
- 2 tablespoons extra-virgin olive oil
- ¼ teaspoon salt
- ⅛ teaspoon freshly ground black pepper
- 1 garlic clove, crushed

Beans:

- 1 pound dried Great Northern beans
- 10 cups water, divided
- 1½ cups coarsely chopped onion
- 1 tablespoon chopped fresh sage
- 1 tablespoon olive oil
- 2 garlic cloves, crushed
- 1 teaspoon salt
- ¼ teaspoon freshly ground black pepper
- 1 cup chopped bottled roasted red bell peppers
- 1 tablespoon balsamic vinegar

1. To prepare pesto, combine first 8 ingredients in a food processor; process until smooth.

2. To prepare beans, sort and wash the beans. Combine beans and 4 cups water in a 6-quart pressure cooker. Close lid securely; bring to high pressure over high heat. Adjust heat to medium or level needed to maintain high pressure, and cook 3 minutes. Remove from heat; place cooker under cold running water. Remove lid; drain beans.

3. Combine beans, 6 cups water, onion, sage, 1 tablespoon olive oil, and 2 garlic cloves in cooker. Close lid securely; bring to high pressure over high heat. Adjust heat to medium or level needed to maintain high pressure; cook 12 minutes. Remove from heat; place cooker under cold running water. Remove lid; let bean mixture stand 10 minutes. Drain bean mixture in a colander over a bowl, reserving 1 cup liquid. Return bean mixture and reserved 1 cup liquid to cooker. Add 1 teaspoon salt, ¼ teaspoon black pepper, bell peppers, and vinegar. Stir well to combine. Top bean mixture with pesto. **Yield: 8 servings (serving size: about ¾ cup bean mixture and 2 tablespoons pesto).**

CALORIES 292; FAT 8g (sat 2.1g, mono 4.1g, poly 1.2g); PROTEIN 16.3g; CARB 40.5g; FIBER 12.7g; CHOL 5mg; IRON 3.9mg; SODIUM 542mg; CALC 212mg

1

2

3

kitchen how-to:
fold a burrito

You'll need large tortillas when making burritos, and you'll want to warm the tortillas before you begin folding to ensure that they are soft and flexible. If you skip this step, the tortillas can crack when you fold them.

1. Lay the tortilla on a flat surface. Spread or spoon the beans (or bean mixture) onto one half of the tortilla, leaving a 1-inch border along the outside edge. Add any other filling ingredients you like, such as fresh salsa, chopped fresh tomato, sautéed tofu, guacamole, and cheese.

2. Fold the edge closest to the filling over the filling (it's OK if the tortilla doesn't completely cover the filling). Fold 1 edge of the tortilla to the side of the filling in toward the filling.

3. Fold the opposite side edge of the tortilla in toward the filling.

4. Holding the folded edges securely, roll the burrito over, covering the filling. Continue rolling until the entire tortilla is used. To serve, place the burrito seam side down to ensure that it doesn't unroll.

4

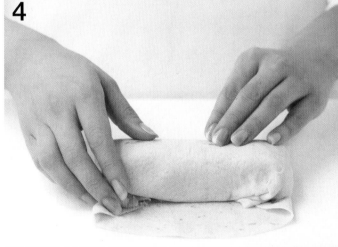

Pinto Bean Nachos

You can use black beans in place of pinto beans, if you prefer. If the bean mixture is too thick, stir in a little hot water.

12 (6-inch) corn tortillas, quartered
Cooking spray
1 tablespoon canola oil
2 teaspoons ground cumin
1 teaspoon chili powder
2 garlic cloves, minced
2 (15-ounce) cans pinto beans, undrained
1 cup (4 ounces) crumbled queso fresco
1 cup bottled salsa
1 cup diced peeled avocado
6 tablespoons chopped fresh cilantro

1. Preheat oven to 425°.
2. Arrange half of tortilla wedges in a single layer on a large baking sheet; lightly coat wedges with cooking spray. Bake at 425° for 8 minutes or until crisp. Repeat procedure with remaining tortilla wedges and cooking spray.
3. Heat oil in a medium saucepan over medium-high heat. Add cumin, chili powder, and garlic; cook 30 seconds, stirring constantly. Add pinto beans, and bring to a boil, stirring frequently. Reduce heat to medium, and simmer 10 minutes. Partially mash bean mixture with a potato masher until slightly thick. Place 8 tortilla chips on each of 6 plates. Spoon about ½ cup bean mixture evenly over tortilla chips on each plate; top each serving with about 2½ tablespoons queso fresco, 2½ tablespoons salsa, and 2½ tablespoons avocado. Sprinkle each serving with 1 tablespoon cilantro. **Yield: 6 servings.**

CALORIES 344; FAT 10.5g (sat 2.2g, mono 4.8g, poly 2.3g); PROTEIN 13.5g; CARB 52.4g; FIBER 11.7g; CHOL 6mg; IRON 3.9mg; SODIUM 723mg; CALC 232mg

kitchen how-to:
make tortilla chips

These freshly baked tortilla chips are sturdy and hold up well under an assortment of toppings. Here we cut 12 (6-inch) tortillas into quarters to yield enough chips for 6 servings.

1. Preheat the oven to 425°. Arrange half of the tortilla wedges in a single layer on a large baking sheet.
2. Lightly coat the wedges with cooking spray.
3. Bake at 425° for 8 minutes or until crisp. Repeat the procedure with the remaining tortilla wedges.

Meatless Crumbles

What they add: Meatless crumbles are generally saturated fat–free and provide a dose of protein. Look for the crumbles near the tofu in the produce section of your supermarket.

Mexican Spices

What they add: Zesty Mexican spices and flavorings sass up plain- or original-flavored meatless crumbles.

Olives

What they add: Olives offer big flavor in a small package. Plus, most of the calories in olives come from heart-healthy monounsaturated fat, which, when replacing saturated fat in the diet, can help lower harmful LDL cholesterol levels.

Mexican Casserole

    4   teaspoons olive oil, divided
    1   cup chopped onion
    2   garlic cloves, minced
    1   jalapeño pepper, minced
    1   teaspoon chili powder
  ½   teaspoon ground cumin
  ¼   teaspoon freshly ground black pepper
    1   (12-ounce) package meatless fat-free crumbles
  48   baked tortilla chips, divided
Cooking spray
    1   (15-ounce) can pinto beans, rinsed and drained
    1   tablespoon fresh lime juice
    2   cups chopped seeded plum tomato
    2   tablespoons minced fresh cilantro
  ¼   teaspoon salt
    1   cup (4 ounces) shredded Monterey Jack cheese
    2   tablespoons fat-free sour cream
    2   tablespoons chopped green onions
  ¼   cup sliced ripe olives

1. Preheat oven to 375°.

2. Heat 2 teaspoons oil in a large nonstick skillet over medium heat. Add onion to pan; cook 4 minutes or until tender. Add garlic and jalapeño; cook 1 minute. Stir in chili powder and next 3 ingredients; cook 3 minutes or until thoroughly heated. Arrange half of tortilla chips in an 11 x 7–inch baking dish coated with cooking spray; top evenly with crumbles mixture.

3. Heat remaining 2 teaspoons oil in skillet over medium heat. Add beans, mashing with the back of a wooden spoon until chunky and thick; cook 2 minutes or until heated, stirring constantly. Stir in lime juice.

4. Combine tomato, cilantro, and salt. Layer beans and tomato mixture over crumbles mixture in dish. Top with remaining tortilla chips, pressing to slightly crush. Sprinkle evenly with cheese. Bake at 375° for 13 minutes or until cheese is bubbly. Cut casserole into 6 equal pieces; top each serving with 1 teaspoon sour cream, 1 teaspoon onions, and 2 teaspoons olives. **Yield: 6 servings.**

CALORIES 313; FAT 12.9g (sat 4.6g, mono 5.2g, poly 2.4g); PROTEIN 20.6g; CARB 30.2g; FIBER 7.4g; CHOL 18mg; IRON 3mg; SODIUM 816mg; CALC 295mg

Polenta with Spinach, Black Beans, and Goat Cheese

1 teaspoon olive oil
2 garlic cloves, minced
½ cup fat-free, less-sodium vegetable broth
   (such as Swanson Certified Organic)
¼ cup chopped drained oil-packed sun-dried
   tomato halves
½ teaspoon ground cumin
1 (15-ounce) can black beans, rinsed and drained
1 (6-ounce) package fresh baby spinach
4 cups water
1 cup uncooked polenta
1 tablespoon butter
½ teaspoon salt
¾ cup (3 ounces) crumbled goat cheese
Cracked black pepper (optional)

1. Heat 1 teaspoon oil in a large nonstick skillet over medium-high heat. Add garlic to pan; sauté 1 minute or until golden. Stir in broth, tomatoes, cumin, and beans; bring to a simmer. Cook 2 minutes, stirring occasionally. Remove from heat. Add spinach, tossing to combine.
2. Bring 4 cups water to a boil in a medium saucepan. Add polenta, butter, and salt; stir well with a whisk. Reduce heat, and simmer 3 minutes or until thick, stirring constantly. Spoon ¾ cup polenta into each of 4 bowls; top each with ¾ cup bean mixture. Sprinkle 3 tablespoons cheese over each serving; garnish with black pepper, if desired. **Yield: 4 servings.**

CALORIES 356; FAT 12g (sat 6.5g, mono 3.6g, poly 1.1g); PROTEIN 13.8g; CARB 48.8g; FIBER 9g; CHOL 24mg; IRON 3.9mg; SODIUM 674mg; CALC 135mg

kitchen how-to: cook polenta

Uncooked polenta provides an easy way to add variety to the dinner repertoire; look for it with other grains in your supermarket or in the baking aisle near the flour.

1. Bring water to a boil in a medium saucepan (4 cups for 1 cup of uncooked polenta is a good ratio). Add the polenta and, if you'd like, butter and salt; stir well with a whisk.

2. Reduce the heat, and simmer 3 minutes or until thick, stirring constantly.

3. Spoon the cooked polenta into a measuring cup to help you portion it.

vegetables

Vegetables are storehouses for a variety of vitamins, minerals, antioxidants, and other healthy compounds. Make them your main dish and bring nutrition to the center of your plate.

Broccoli
What it adds: Broccoli is one of the best vegetable sources of calcium. A short boil of the broccoli preserves the bright color for the dish.

Dijon Mustard:
What it adds: The mustard boosts the savory quality of this dish.

Béchamel Sauce
What it adds: The béchamel sauce, thickened with cheese, boosts the calcium even more.

Stuffed Portobello Mushrooms

While panko (Japanese) breadcrumbs (available in the Asian foods aisle at most supermarkets) work best in this dish, you can substitute freshly made coarse breadcrumbs, if necessary. Two colors of tomato give it a nice presentation, but you can use all red or yellow, too.

 4 (6-inch) portobello mushrooms, stems removed
Cooking spray
 1 cup chopped red tomato
 1 cup chopped yellow tomato
 1 cup panko (Japanese) breadcrumbs
 1 cup (4 ounces) preshredded part-skim
     mozzarella cheese
 ¼ cup chopped fresh chives
 ¼ teaspoon salt
 ¼ teaspoon black pepper

1. Preheat broiler.
2. Remove brown gills from undersides of mushrooms using a spoon; discard gills. Place mushrooms, gill sides down, on a foil-lined baking sheet coated with cooking spray. Broil mushrooms 5 minutes.
3. While mushrooms broil, combine tomatoes and next 3 ingredients.
4. Turn mushrooms over, and sprinkle evenly with salt and pepper. Divide tomato mixture evenly among mushrooms. Broil 5 minutes or until cheese melts. **Yield: 4 servings (serving size: 1 stuffed mushroom).**

CALORIES 184; FAT 5.3g (sat 2.9g, mono 1.3g, poly 0.2g); PROTEIN 12.6g; CARB 21.6g; FIBER 3.5g; CHOL 16mg; IRON 1.3mg; SODIUM 325mg; CALC 209mg

kitchen how-to:
degill portobellos

Holding 1 portobello in your hand, use a spoon or butter knife to carefully scrape away the dark brown gills on the underside.

{vegan recipe}

Potato Roti Curry

This mild, soupy side dish hails from the Caribbean, where it's often made with sweet calabaza squash and served alongside or stuffed into the tortilla-like Indian flatbread roti. While roti is traditional, whole-wheat tortillas or pitas are great accompaniments for sopping up the liquid. Serve this dish with lime wedges and rice.

1¼ teaspoons salt
2 teaspoons ground cumin
1½ teaspoons ground turmeric
1 teaspoon ground ginger
¼ teaspoon ground allspice
¼ teaspoon crushed red pepper
1 tablespoon canola oil
1½ cups chopped onion
4 garlic cloves, minced
4 cups (1-inch) cubed peeled Yukon gold potato (about 1½ pounds)
3 cups (1-inch) cubed peeled acorn squash (about ¾ pound)
1 cup chopped red bell pepper
2 cups water
½ cup light coconut milk
½ cup chopped fresh cilantro

1. Combine first 6 ingredients; set aside.
2. Heat oil in a large Dutch oven over medium heat. Add onion; cook 3 minutes or until tender, stirring frequently. Add garlic; cook 15 seconds, stirring constantly. Add spice mixture; cook 30 seconds, stirring constantly. Add potato, squash, and bell pepper, stirring to coat with spice mixture; cook 1 minute, stirring constantly. Stir in water and coconut milk, scraping pan to loosen browned bits; bring to a boil. Cover, reduce heat, and simmer 25 minutes or until potato is tender. Sprinkle with cilantro. **Yield: 6 servings (serving size: about 1 cup).**

CALORIES 183; FAT 3.9g (sat 1.2g, mono 1.4g, poly 0.9g); PROTEIN 3.6g; CARB 36.2g; FIBER 4.1g; CHOL 0mg; IRON 1.7mg; SODIUM 510mg; CALC 56mg

kitchen how-to:
peel & cube acorn squash

To easily peel and cube acorn squash, first pierce the shell of the squash in several places with a fork, and then microwave at HIGH for 2 minutes. Let the squash cool slightly before peeling it.

1. Using a vegetable peeler, carefully remove the skin of the squash.
2. Once the squash is peeled, cut it in half, and scoop out the seeds using a spoon or your fingers. Cut it into 1-inch pieces, and chop or dice it, depending on the recipe directions.

Spaghetti Squash with Edamame-Cilantro Pesto

Prepare and chill the pesto up to two days ahead, and bring it to room temperature before serving. Bake and chill the squash halves a day or two before; it's actually easier to remove the flesh when it's cold. Reheat the cold squash in the microwave. This unique pesto would also be good on a pizza with sun-dried tomatoes.

  2 **(2½-pound) spaghetti squash**
    Cooking spray
  ½ **teaspoon salt, divided**
1¼ **cups chopped fresh cilantro**
  1 **cup vegetable broth**
  1 **tablespoon extra-virgin olive oil**
  ¼ **teaspoon freshly ground black pepper**
  2 **garlic cloves, minced**
  1 **pound frozen shelled edamame (green soybeans), thawed**
  ¼ **cup (1 ounce) grated fresh Parmesan cheese**

1. Preheat oven to 350°.
2. Cut each squash in half lengthwise; discard seeds. Place squash halves, cut sides down, on a baking sheet coated with cooking spray. Bake at 350° for 1 hour or until tender. Cool slightly. Scrape inside of squash with a fork to remove spaghetti-like strands to measure about 8 cups. Place in a large bowl. Sprinkle with ¼ teaspoon salt; toss gently to combine. Cover and keep warm.
3. Place cilantro, broth, oil, pepper, remaining ¼ teaspoon salt, garlic, and edamame in a food processor; pulse until coarsely chopped. Serve edamame pesto over squash; sprinkle with cheese. **Yield: 6 servings (serving size: 1½ cups squash, ½ cup edamame pesto, and 2 teaspoons cheese).**

CALORIES 233; FAT 7.6g (sat 1.3g, mono 2.8g, poly 2.4g); PROTEIN 12.5g; CARB 31.3g; FIBER 8.8g; CHOL 3mg; IRON 3mg; SODIUM 533mg; CALC 182mg

kitchen how-to: prepare spaghetti squash

This melon-shaped winter squash is named for its flesh, which separates into spaghetti-like strands after it's cooked. When buying, choose a hard squash with smooth pale yellow or ivory skin.

1. Preheat the oven to 350°. Cut each squash in half lengthwise.

2. Scoop away the seeds. Place the squash halves, cut sides down, on a baking sheet coated with cooking spray. Bake at 350° for 1 hour or until tender when pierced with a fork.

3. Cool slightly. Hold the squash in a vertical position with one hand, and use a fork to gently scrape out the spaghetti-like flesh, working from the top to the base.

Swiss Chard Spanakopita Casserole

Cooking spray
2¼ cups minced white onion
¾ cup minced green onions
3 garlic cloves, minced
9 cups chopped trimmed Swiss chard (about 1½ pounds)
6 tablespoons chopped fresh parsley
3 tablespoons minced fresh mint
1 cup (4 ounces) crumbled feta cheese
½ cup (2 ounces) freshly grated Parmesan cheese
½ teaspoon salt
¼ teaspoon black pepper
3 large egg whites
10 (18 x 14–inch) sheets frozen phyllo dough, thawed

1. Preheat oven to 350°.
2. Heat a large nonstick skillet coated with cooking spray over medium-high heat. Add white onion; sauté 7 minutes or until golden. Add green onions and garlic, and sauté 1 minute. Stir in chard; cook 2 minutes or until chard wilts. Stir in parsley and mint, and cook 1 minute. Place in a large bowl; cool slightly. Stir in feta cheese and next 4 ingredients.
3. Place 1 phyllo sheet on a large cutting board (cover remaining phyllo to prevent drying), and coat with cooking spray. Top with 1 phyllo sheet, and coat with cooking spray. Repeat procedure with 3 additional sheets (stack should contain 5 phyllo sheets).
4. Cut phyllo stack into a 14-inch square. Place square in center of a 13 x 9–inch baking dish coated with cooking spray, allowing phyllo to extend up long sides of dish. Cut 14 x 4–inch piece of stacked phyllo into 2 (7 x 4–inch) rectangles. Fold each 7 x 4–inch rectangle in half lengthwise. Place a folded rectangle against each short side of dish. Spread chard mixture evenly over phyllo. Repeat Step 3 with remaining 5 phyllo sheets. Place 18 x 14–inch phyllo stack over chard mixture. Fold phyllo edges into center. Coat with cooking spray. Score phyllo by making 2 lengthwise cuts and 3 crosswise cuts to form 12 rectangles. Bake at 350° for 40 minutes or until golden. Yield: 12 servings (serving size: 1 rectangle).

CALORIES 121; FAT 4.7g (sat 2.8g, mono 1.4g, poly 0.3g); PROTEIN 6.1g; CARB 13.6g; FIBER 1.6g; CHOL 14mg; IRON 1.3mg; SODIUM 449mg; CALC 134mg

kitchen how-to:
arrange phyllo for Swiss chard spanakopita casserole

1

2

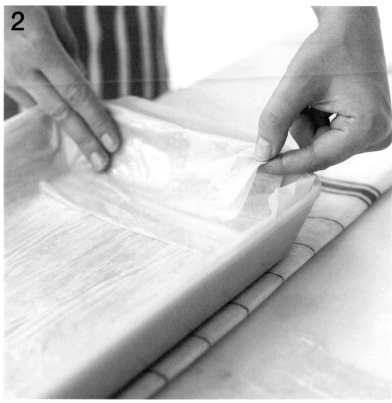

To get started in the assembly of this dish, place 1 phyllo sheet on a large cutting board (cover the remaining phyllo to prevent drying), and coat it with cooking spray. Top with 1 additional phyllo sheet, and coat with cooking spray. Repeat the procedure with 3 additional sheets (the stack should contain 5 phyllo sheets).

1. Cut the phyllo stack into a 14-inch square. Place the square in the center of a 13 x 9–inch baking dish coated with cooking spray, allowing the phyllo to extend up the long sides of the dish. Cut the 14 x 4–inch piece of the stacked phyllo into 2 (7 x 4–inch) rectangles.

2. Fold each 7 x 4–inch rectangle in half lengthwise. Place a folded rectangle against each short side of the dish. Spread the chard mixture evenly over the phyllo. Place 1 phyllo sheet on a large cutting board (cover the remaining phyllo to prevent drying), and coat it with cooking spray. Top with 1 phyllo sheet, and

coat it with cooking spray. Repeat the procedure with the remaining 3 phyllo sheets. Place the 18 x 14–inch phyllo stack over the chard mixture. Fold the phyllo edges into the center. Coat the phyllo with cooking spray. Score the phyllo by making 2 lengthwise cuts and 3 crosswise cuts to form 12 rectangles. Bake.

Deep-Dish Roasted Vegetable Pizza

3.6 ounces whole-wheat flour (about ¾ cup)

3.4 ounces all-purpose flour (about ¾ cup)

1 package quick-rise yeast (about 2¼ teaspoons)

½ teaspoon salt

½ teaspoon sugar

⅔ cup very warm water (120° to 130°)

1 tablespoon olive oil

Olive oil–flavored cooking spray

1 medium-size green bell pepper, cut into 1-inch pieces

1 (8-ounce) package baby portobello mushrooms, halved

1 medium-size red onion, cut into 1-inch pieces

1 teaspoon dried Italian seasoning

½ cup pitted kalamata olives, halved

4 plum tomatoes, coarsely chopped

2 cups (8 ounces) shredded part-skim mozzarella cheese, divided

½ cup spicy marinara sauce (such as Barilla)

1. Preheat oven to 475°.

2. Weigh or lightly spoon flours into dry measuring cups; level with a knife. Place flours, yeast, salt, and sugar in a food processor; pulse 2 times or until blended. Combine very warm water and oil in a 1-cup glass measure. With processor on, slowly pour water mixture through food chute; process until mixture forms a ball. Process 1 minute. Turn dough out onto a floured surface; coat dough with cooking spray. Let rest 15 minutes.

3. While dough rests, combine bell pepper, mushrooms, and onion on a large rimmed baking sheet. Coat vegetables with cooking spray; sprinkle with Italian seasoning, and toss well. Bake at 475° for 20 minutes; stir, and bake an additional 6 minutes or until vegetables are roasted. Add olives and tomato to vegetables; toss gently.

4. Reduce oven temperature to 450°.

5. Roll dough into a 14 x 10–inch rectangle on a lightly floured surface. Coat a 13 x 9–inch baking pan with cooking spray. Place dough in prepared pan, and press dough halfway up sides of pan. Sprinkle ¾ cup cheese over dough; spread marinara sauce over cheese. Top with roasted vegetable mixture. Sprinkle with remaining 1¼ cups cheese. Bake at 450° for 20 minutes or until crust browns and cheese bubbles. Cool 5 minutes before cutting into squares. **Yield: 6 servings (serving size: 1 square).**

CALORIES 332; FAT 14.3g (sat 5.6g, mono 6.3g, poly 1.1g); PROTEIN 16.6g; CARB 36.4g; FIBER 4.7g; CHOL 20mg; IRON 2.4mg; SODIUM 678mg; CALC 307mg

kitchen how-to: make deep-dish pizza

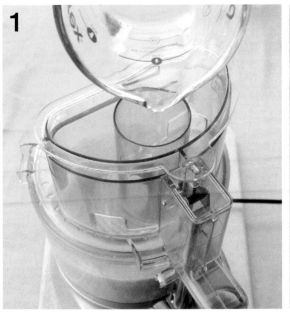

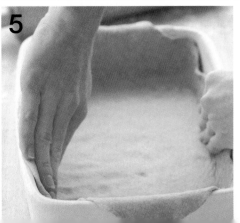

Deep-dish pizza is the archetypal Chicago food. Our version of this classic food reduces the amount of oil that's typically found in a deep-dish crust. We sprinkle a bit of mozzarella on the top, although most traditional deep-dish pies keep the cheese on the bottom in a thick, oozing layer.

1. Weigh or lightly spoon the flours into dry measuring cups; level with a knife. Place the flours, yeast, salt, and sugar in a food processor; pulse 2 times or until blended. Combine very warm water and oil in a 1-cup glass measure. With the processor on, slowly pour the water mixture through the food chute.

2. Process until mixture forms a ball. Process 1 minute.

3. Turn the dough out onto a floured surface; coat the dough with cooking spray. Let it rest for 15 minutes.

4. Roll the dough into a 14 x 10–inch rectangle on a lightly floured surface.

5. Coat a 13 x 9–inch baking pan with cooking spray. Place the dough in the prepared pan; press dough halfway up the sides of the pan. Add the filling and cheese layers according to the recipe's directions. Bake.

Pesto

What it adds: This blend of basil, nuts, Parmesan cheese, garlic, and olive oil provides a rich punch of herbal flavor to this pizza.

Pecorino Romano Cheese

What it adds: This aromatic sheep's milk cheese has a pleasantly sharp taste.

Zucchini, Olive, and Cheese Quesadillas

1 teaspoon olive oil
Cooking spray
⅓ cup finely chopped onion
½ teaspoon bottled minced garlic
1¼ cups shredded zucchini
¼ teaspoon dried oregano
⅛ teaspoon salt
⅛ teaspoon black pepper
4 (8-inch) fat-free flour tortillas
½ cup (2 ounces) preshredded part-skim
    mozzarella cheese, divided
½ cup diced tomato, divided
¼ cup chopped pitted kalamata olives, divided
¼ cup (1 ounce) crumbled feta cheese, divided

1. Heat olive oil in a large nonstick skillet coated with cooking spray over medium-high heat. Add onion and garlic; sauté 1 minute. Add zucchini; sauté 2 minutes or until lightly browned. Remove from heat; stir in oregano, salt, and pepper.

2. Wipe pan clean with paper towels, and coat with cooking spray. Heat pan over medium heat. Add 1 tortilla to pan, and sprinkle with ¼ cup mozzarella. Top with half of zucchini mixture, ¼ cup tomato, 2 tablespoons olives, 2 tablespoons feta, and 1 tortilla. Cook 3 minutes or until lightly browned on bottom. Carefully turn quesadilla; cook 2 minutes or until lightly browned. Place quesadilla on a cutting board; cut in half using a serrated knife. Repeat procedure with remaining tortillas, mozzarella, zucchini mixture, tomato, olives, and feta. Serve warm. **Yield: 4 servings.**

CALORIES 235; FAT 7.9g (sat 3.6g, mono 3.1g, poly 0.5g); PROTEIN 8.7g; CARB 23.7g; FIBER 3.8g; CHOL 14mg; IRON 0.7mg; SODIUM 632mg; CALC 160mg

kitchen how-to: make quesadillas

Basic quesadillas are corn or flour tortillas filled with cheese and then cooked until the cheese melts. You can add any other ingredients you like, but since the cook time in the pan is relatively short, you'll need to cook your filling ingredients first.

1. Sauté the filling ingredients in olive oil or cooking spray until lightly browned. Remove from the heat.
2. Wipe the pan clean with paper towels, and coat it with cooking spray.
3. Heat the pan over medium heat. Add 1 tortilla to the pan, and sprinkle it with cheese.

4. Top with half of the sautéed filling ingredients, and add any additional ingredients you like, such as fresh chopped tomatoes, olives, or cheese.
5. Cook for 3 minutes or until lightly browned on bottom. Carefully turn over the quesadilla.
6. Cook it for 2 minutes or until lightly browned.
7. Place the quesadilla on a cutting board; cut it into wedges using a serrated knife. Repeat the procedure with the remaining tortillas and filling.

Corn and Chile Quesadillas

If you can't find fresh Anaheim chiles, substitute about ¼ cup chopped canned green chiles. Sharp cheddar or aged Gruyère cheese could stand in for the Gouda, if you prefer.

- 2 Anaheim chiles (about ½ pound)
- 2 teaspoons olive oil
- 1 cup thinly sliced shiitake mushroom caps (about 1¼ ounces)
- 1 cup frozen whole-kernel corn, thawed
- ¼ cup chopped green onions
- ⅛ teaspoon salt
- ⅛ teaspoon ground black pepper
- 1 cup (4 ounces) shredded aged Gouda cheese
- 4 (8-inch) flour tortillas
- Cooking spray
- ½ cup bottled salsa

1. Preheat broiler.

2. Cut chiles in half lengthwise; discard seeds and membranes. Place chile halves, skin sides up, on a foil-lined baking sheet; flatten with hand. Broil 8 minutes or until blackened. Place in a zip-top plastic bag; seal. Let stand 15 minutes. Peel and chop. Reduce oven temperature to 200°.

3. Heat oil in a large nonstick skillet over medium-high heat. Add mushrooms; sauté 2 minutes. Add corn and next 3 ingredients; sauté 2 minutes. Place mixture in a bowl; stir in chopped chiles. Wipe pan clean.

4. Place about ¼ cup mushroom mixture and ¼ cup cheese over half of 1 tortilla. Repeat procedure with remaining 1¼ cups mushroom mixture, remaining ¾ cup cheese, and remaining 3 tortillas. Heat pan over medium heat; coat pan with cooking spray. Place 1 tortilla in pan; cook 2 minutes or until cheese melts and bottom is golden. Fold tortilla in half; place on a baking sheet. Place in 200° oven to keep warm. Repeat procedure with remaining tortillas. Cut each quesadilla into wedges; serve with salsa. **Yield: 4 servings (serving size: 1 quesadilla and 2 tablespoons salsa).**

CALORIES 341; FAT 15.1g (sat 6.7g, mono 6.1g, poly 1.5g); PROTEIN 13.6g; CARB 39.5g; FIBER 4.4g; CHOL 25mg; IRON 2.7mg; SODIUM 738mg; CALC 293mg

kitchen how-to: broil chiles

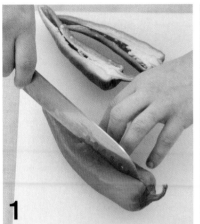

Broiling gives chile peppers a soft, silky texture and adds a smoky flavor to their heat. Lining the baking sheet with foil makes cleanup a cinch.

1. Preheat the broiler. Cut the chiles in half lengthwise.
2. Discard the seeds and membranes.
3. Place the chile halves, skin sides up, on a foil-lined baking sheet.
4. Flatten each chile with your hand.
5. Broil the chiles 8 minutes or until blackened. Place them in a zip-top plastic bag; seal. Let them stand 15 minutes.
6. Peel and chop the chiles.

way to cook vegetarian

tofu
& tempeh

tofu & tempeh

Tofu and tempeh have a lot in common. Their flavor, texture, and high protein content make both of them excellent bases for hearty vegetarian meals. They work in an array of culinary applications, too, including sautéing, baking, roasting, and steaming, which can help keep your taste buds happy.

Tofu

Neutral-tasting tofu is known for readily absorbing flavor from other ingredients. It adapts to any flavor profile and works in a variety of cooking methods. Nutritionally, it supplies protein and heart-healthy fats. Plus, if you buy a variety containing calcium sulfate, you can also get a dose of calcium. You'll need to look carefully at the nutrition label to verify that the tofu you are buying is made with calcium sulfate. Nigari (magnesium chloride) is another common coagulating agent used to make tofu, but it has a lower calcium content—4 ounces of tofu made with nigari has about 200 milligrams of calcium compared to 600 milligrams found in 4 ounces of tofu made with calcium sulfate. Once opened, refrigerate tofu and use it within three to four days. When storing water-packed tofu, you'll need to place it in an airtight container and cover it with water; change the water daily to keep it fresh.

Tofu Varieties

The main consideration with tofu is matching the type to the recipe.
Silken tofu: As the name implies, this type of tofu has a soft, smooth texture. It's a soy milk that's simply thickened with a coagulant, and although packages are often labeled *soft, firm,* and *extra-firm,* you shouldn't rely on this tofu to hold its shape in a vigorously cooked dish like a stir-fry.
Water-packed tofu: In a process similar to that of making cheese, soy milk is heated, and salts are added to separate the milk into curds and whey. To make blocks of tofu, the curds are scooped out, pressed into molds, and drained. Use water-packed tofu in stir-fries and

other savory applications where you want it to hold its shape after it's cooked. You'll need to rinse water-packed tofu before you cook it.

Flavored tofu: Tofus can be infused with herbs and spices to produce a wide variety of flavors—from teriyaki and curry to Mediter-ranean. You'll also find varieties that are baked or steamed with a liquid, such as soy sauce, to produce a savory product that doesn't require any other preparation. You'll usually find these precooked varieties in vacuum-sealed packaging.

Tempeh

Tempeh (pronounced TEHM-pay) is made by a simple process—hull soybeans, crack and boil them, and then introduce a starter bacteria that ferments the soybean mixture. The result is a pebbled, buff-colored soybean cake. That minimal processing helps tempeh retain many of the nutritional properties related to soybeans, such as high-quality protein, fiber, and calcium, and it can also provide significant amounts of iron.

Tempeh has an assertive flavor. It obtains much of its nutty, subtle, tangy flavor from the fermentation process. When the temperature changes, the bacteria present in tempeh may cause small patches of gray or black spores to bloom on the surface of the cake. These spores are harmless and only add to tempeh's unique yeasty flavor. You can store opened tempeh, tightly wrapped, in the refrigerator for up to five days.

Tempeh Varieties

Three-grain, wild rice, and plain soy tempeh are generally inter-changeable. Here are the basic flavor profiles of tempeh varieties available at grocery stores and health-food stores.

1. Wild rice: This crunchy version imparts a black olive undertone. You can use it crumbled in Italian red sauces, a roasted vegetable dish, or with sweet-and-sour Asian dishes.

2. Soy: A pleasing chewy texture gives way to the characteristic tang of the soy cake. This tempeh works best marinated or with a flavorful herb, spice, or nut sauce.

3. Flax: This variety has sub-stantial bite, but it's a bit dry. Flax tempeh works well in breakfast casseroles or marinated and simmered in a rich broth or tangy sauce.

4. Garden vegetable: Carrots and bell peppers give this tempeh bouillon undertones. Grate some garden vegetable tempeh to use as "croutons" on a salad or add it to vegetable noodle soup.

5. Multigrain: With a combina-tion of millet, soybeans, brown rice, barley, or oats, these varieties have a mild taste that could pair well with any flavoring—barbe-cued, as a fajita filler, or even in a potpie.

6. Original: This variety has a crunchy and chewy bite and mild nutty flavor.

1
2
3
4
5
6

tofu

Tofu is amazingly versatile and adaptable. It absorbs the flavors of the ingredients it's paired with and works in a variety of cooking methods.

Peanut-Crusted Tofu Triangles

    1   (14-ounce) package firm tofu, drained
 1½   cups uncooked instant rice
 1½   cups rice milk
   ½   cup thinly sliced green onions
   ⅓   cup chopped fresh cilantro
    3   tablespoons finely chopped red bell pepper
    1   teaspoon salt, divided
    1   teaspoon water
    1   large egg white
   ⅓   cup dry-roasted peanuts
   ½   teaspoon garlic powder
   ½   teaspoon ground ginger
   ½   teaspoon crushed red pepper
    2   teaspoons peanut oil, divided
        Cooking spray

1. Cut tofu crosswise into 8 equal pieces; cut each
piece into two triangles. Arrange tofu in a single layer on
several layers of heavy-duty paper towels; cover tofu
with additional paper towels. Place a heavy pan on top.
Let stand 20 minutes. Pat tofu dry with paper towels.
2. Combine rice and rice milk in a medium saucepan;
bring to a boil. Cover, reduce heat, and simmer 5 minutes. Stir in onions, cilantro, bell pepper, and ½ teaspoon
salt. Cover and keep warm.
3. Combine 1 teaspoon water and egg white in a shallow
dish. Place peanuts in a food processor; process until
finely ground. Combine ground peanuts, garlic powder,
ginger, red pepper, and remaining ½ teaspoon salt in a
shallow dish. Dip one side of each tofu triangle in egg
mixture; dredge the same side in peanut mixture. Heat
1 teaspoon oil in a large nonstick skillet coated with cooking spray over medium heat. Add half of tofu; cook 2
minutes on each side or until browned (watch closely to
prevent burning). Repeat procedure with remaining 1 teaspoon oil and tofu. Serve tofu with rice. **Yield: 4 servings
(serving size: ¾ cup rice and 4 tofu triangles).**

CALORIES 391; FAT 15.1g (sat 2.5g, mono 5.5g, poly 6.6g); PROTEIN 17.6g; CARB 46.7g;
FIBER 2.6g; CHOL 0mg; IRON 3.1mg; SODIUM 748mg; CALC 101mg

kitchen how-to: press tofu

Tofu is generally packaged in water to keep the
product fresh. It's best to remove some of that water
from the medium, firm, and extra-firm varieties before
marinating and sautéing or stir-frying it to remove excess
moisture so the tofu will brown more easily.

1. Remove the tofu from the package, and cut it into
slices for easier draining.
2. Lay each slice flat on a few absorbent heavy-duty
paper towels.
3. Top with another layer of paper towels; place a heavy
pan on top.
4. Let it stand for 30 minutes, pressing occasionally to
release excess water.

Tofu Steaks with Red Pepper-Walnut Sauce

The herb-flecked marinade also serves as the base of a delicious Mediterranean-style dipping sauce. Serve this dish with couscous or toasted bread to enjoy all of the sauce.

- 1   (14-ounce) package water-packed reduced-fat extra-firm tofu
- ¼   cup finely chopped fresh basil
- ¼   cup water
- 2   tablespoons chopped fresh parsley
- 1   tablespoon chopped fresh thyme
- 2   tablespoons white wine vinegar
- 1   tablespoon Dijon mustard
- ½   teaspoon salt
- ½   teaspoon crushed red pepper
- 8   garlic cloves, minced
- ½   cup all-purpose flour
- ½   cup egg substitute
- 2   cups panko (Japanese breadcrumbs)
- 2   tablespoons olive oil
- 3   tablespoons chopped walnuts, toasted
- 1   (12-ounce) bottle roasted red peppers, drained

1. Cut tofu crosswise into 4 slices. Place tofu slices on several layers of heavy-duty paper towels; cover with additional paper towels. Let stand 30 minutes, pressing down occasionally.

2. Combine basil and next 8 ingredients in a large zip-top plastic bag. Add tofu to bag; seal. Marinate in refrigerator 1 hour, turning bag occasionally.

3. Place flour in a shallow dish. Place egg substitute in another shallow dish. Place panko in another shallow dish.

4. Remove tofu from marinade, reserving remaining marinade. Working with one tofu piece at a time, dredge tofu in flour, shaking off excess. Dip tofu in egg substitute, allowing excess to drip off. Coat tofu completely with panko, pressing lightly to adhere.

Set aside. Repeat procedure with remaining tofu, flour, egg substitute, and panko.

5. Heat a large nonstick skillet over medium-high heat. Add olive oil to pan, swirling to coat. Add tofu to pan; reduce heat to medium, and cook 4 minutes on each side or until browned. Remove tofu from pan, and keep warm.

6. Combine reserved marinade, walnuts, and bell peppers in a blender; process until smooth (about 2 minutes). Pour bell pepper mixture into pan; cook over medium-high heat 2 minutes or until thoroughly heated. Serve with tofu. **Yield: 4 servings (serving size: 1 tofu piece and about ⅓ cup sauce).**

CALORIES 291; FAT 15.1g (sat 1.3g, mono 6.4g, poly 5.9g); PROTEIN 15.9g; CARB 23g; FIBER 3.5g; CHOL 0mg; IRON 2.8mg; SODIUM 661mg; CALC 74mg

kitchen how-to:
bread &
pan-fry tofu

Most of our breaded recipes use a three-step approach: The food is first dusted in flour to help all the other coatings cling, then dipped into an egg wash to help the main coating adhere, and finally dredged in the main/heavier coating. You'll find it helpful to designate one hand as the dry hand (for handling the food as it goes into the dry ingredients) and the other as the wet hand (for dipping food into the egg wash); if you use the same hand or both hands for every step, you'll end up with a mess of flour-egg-breadcrumbs stuck to your skin. Don't let the food sit too long after it's breaded or it can become gummy.

1. Working with 1 tofu piece at a time, dredge the tofu in the flour, shaking off the excess.
2. Dip the tofu in the egg wash, allowing the excess to drip off.
3. Coat the tofu completely with the coating mixture.
4. Press the mixture into the tofu lightly to adhere; set it aside. Repeat the procedure with the remaining tofu, flour, egg wash, and bread-crumb mixture.
5. Heat a large nonstick skillet over medium-high heat. Add oil to the pan, swirling to coat. Add the tofu to the pan; reduce the heat to medium.
6. Cook the tofu for 4 minutes on each side or until browned. Remove the tofu from the pan.

Reduced-Sodium Tamari
What it adds: Using a reduced-sodium variety of tamari saves more than 300 milligrams of sodium per tablespoon.

Mix of Flours
What they add: The batter is made with all-purpose flour, which adheres well because it contains gluten, but too much causes the food to absorb more oil. Adding gluten-free ingredients like rice flour reduces oil absorption.

Club Soda
What it adds: Adding club soda to the batter produces gas bubbles that discourage oil absorption.

{vegan recipe}

Tempura Tofu and Spring Vegetables

1 (14-ounce) package water-packed extra-firm
  tofu, drained
12 cups peanut oil
6 tablespoons rice vinegar
1½ tablespoons sugar
3 tablespoons reduced-sodium tamari
1½ teaspoons grated peeled fresh ginger
1 pound baby carrots with green tops
4.5 ounces all-purpose flour (about 1 cup)
6.75 ounces rice flour (about 1 cup)
1 teaspoon baking soda
½ teaspoon salt
2 cups club soda, chilled
12 ounces sugar snap peas, trimmed

1. Place tofu on several layers of paper towels; cover
with paper towels. Top with a heavy skillet; let stand
30 minutes. Discard paper towels. Cut tofu in half
horizontally; cut blocks into 16 (½-inch-thick) slices.
Cut slices in half, crosswise, to form 32 (1 x ½–inch)
rectangles.
2. Clip a candy/fry thermometer onto the side of a
large pan; add oil to pan. Heat oil to 385°. Combine

vinegar and next 3 ingredients. Trim carrot tops to
1 inch; peel carrots.
3. Weigh or lightly spoon flours into dry measuring cups;
level with a knife. Combine flours, baking soda, and salt,
stirring well with a whisk. Gradually add club soda,
stirring until smooth. Using a slotted spoon, dip tofu
in batter. Place tofu in hot oil, and fry 1 minute or until
golden, turning once. Make sure oil temperature remains
at 375°. Remove tofu, and drain.
4. Return oil temperature to 385°. Using a slotted spoon,
dip carrots in batter. Place carrots in oil; fry 2 minutes
or until golden, turning once. Make sure oil temperature
remains at 375°. Remove carrots; drain. Return oil
temperature to 385°.
5. Using a slotted spoon, dip peas in batter. Place
peas in oil; fry 1 minute or until golden, turning once.
Make sure oil temperature remains at 375°. Remove
peas; drain. Serve tofu and vegetables with tamari
mixture. **Yield: 5 servings (serving size: about 6
tofu pieces, 5 carrots, 7 peas, and 2½ tablespoons
dipping sauce).**

CALORIES 428; FAT 19.4g (sat 3g, mono 10.2g, poly 5.2g); PROTEIN 12.9g; CARB 46.2g;
FIBER 4.9g; CHOL 0mg; IRON 3.5mg; SODIUM 826mg; CALC 201mg

kitchen how-to: fry in a healthier way

Fried foods can have a place in a healthy diet.
Science shows that proper frying minimizes oil absorption while creating that sublime, toasty crust we all love.
Choose a healthy oil that's low in saturated fat. We use
peanut oil, but soybean and canola oils are also good
options. You'll want to fry in a large pan like a deep
skillet or Dutch oven to avoid overcrowding. You need
to watch the temperature like a hawk, so be sure to
clip a fry thermometer to the side of the pan. Watch
the thermometer, and slow the pace or adjust the
heat as needed. Too-hot oil will burn the exterior
before the interior is fully cooked. Oil that's not hot
enough will slow the cooking process and also soak
up extra oil—making the food greasy and soggy.

{ vegan recipe }

Pan-Crisped Tofu with Greens and Peanut Dressing

⅓ cup white miso (soybean paste)
⅓ cup mirin (sweet rice wine)
⅓ cup rice vinegar
1 tablespoon finely grated peeled fresh ginger
½ cup chopped dry-roasted peanuts, divided
5 tablespoons canola oil, divided
2 (14-ounce) packages water-packed firm tofu, drained
8 cups gourmet salad greens
Minced fresh chives (optional)

1. Combine first 4 ingredients, ¼ cup peanuts, and 3 tablespoons oil in a small bowl; stir with a whisk.
2. Cut each tofu block crosswise into 8 (½-inch-thick) slices. Arrange tofu on several layers of paper towels.

Top with several more layers of paper towels; top with a cast-iron skillet or other heavy pan. Let stand 30 minutes. Remove tofu from paper towels.
3. Heat 1 tablespoon oil in a large nonstick skillet over medium-high heat. Add 8 tofu slices to pan; sauté 4 minutes on each side or until crisp and golden. Remove from pan, and drain tofu on paper towels. Repeat procedure with remaining 1 tablespoon oil and remaining 8 tofu slices. Place 1 cup greens on each of 8 plates. Top each serving with 2 tofu slices, 3 tablespoons miso mixture, and 1½ teaspoons chopped peanuts. Garnish each serving with chives, if desired.
Yield: 8 servings.

CALORIES 266; FAT 18g (sat 1.8g, mono 8.3g, poly 6.8g); PROTEIN 13.9g; CARB 13g; FIBER 4.1g; CHOL 0mg; IRON 3mg; SODIUM 375mg; CALC 227mg

kitchen how-to: sauté tofu

Sautéing tofu cubes gives them a nice firm texture and caramelized flavor.

1. Heat oil in a large nonstick skillet over medium-high heat.
2. Add ½-inch-thick tofu slices to pan (you'll get 8 slices per one 14-ounce package of water-packed firm tofu).
3. Sauté 4 minutes on each side or until the tofu is crisp and golden.
4. Remove the crisped tofu from the pan, and drain it on paper towels.

{ vegan recipe }

Sweet Hot Tofu

With the tofu coated in an assertive sauce, this dish will win over even the pickiest eaters. Use bottled ginger and garlic to save time, and serve the flavorful concoction over steaming white rice.

- 1 (3½-ounce) bag boil-in-bag long-grain rice
- 2 teaspoons canola oil
- 1 (14-ounce) package firm reduced-fat tofu, cut into (1-inch) cubes
- ⅔ cup organic vegetable broth (such as Swanson Certified Organic)
- ¼ cup hoisin sauce
- 1 tablespoon sherry
- 1 teaspoon cornstarch
- 2 teaspoons less-sodium soy sauce
- 1 teaspoon honey
- ½ teaspoon dark sesame oil
- Dash of crushed red pepper
- 2 teaspoons bottled minced fresh ginger
- 2 teaspoons bottled minced garlic
- ⅓ cup thinly sliced green onions

1. Prepare rice according to package directions, omitting salt and fat.
2. Heat canola oil in a large nonstick skillet over medium-high heat. Add tofu, and sauté 5 minutes or until lightly browned. Remove from skillet.
3. Combine broth and next 7 ingredients, stirring well with a whisk.
4. Add ginger, garlic, and onions to pan; sauté 30 seconds. Stir in broth mixture; cook 1 minute or until thickened, stirring constantly. Add tofu to pan; cook 30 seconds, stirring gently to coat. Divide rice evenly among each of 4 plates; top each serving with tofu mixture. **Yield: 4 servings (serving size: about ½ cup rice and about ½ cup tofu mixture).**

CALORIES 275; FAT 7.9g (sat 1g, mono 2.8g, poly 3.9g); PROTEIN 14.1g; CARB 36.1g; FIBER 3.2g; CHOL 0.5mg; IRON 2.6mg; SODIUM 425mg; CALC 55mg

Canola Oil
What it adds: With the lowest amount of saturated fat of any cooking oil, canola helps keep this quick sauté in line nutritionally.

Less-Sodium Soy Sauce
What it adds: Compared to regular soy sauce, the less-sodium variety saves more than 300 milligrams of sodium per tablespoon.

Reduced-Fat Tofu

What it adds: The reduced-fat variety helps keep the fat content of this dish low. Regular tofu gets 57 percent of its calories from fat, while reduced-fat gets 26 percent from fat. Make the switch in other recipes if you like—we find the flavor to be just as delicious and versatile.

Potatoes

What they add: Prepackaged diced potatoes help speed the preparation of this comforting meal. They also add fiber and a healthy dose of potassium.

Asparagus

What it adds: These slender shoots add color and crispness to this stir-fry. Plus, green asparagus is higher in vitamins A and C and folate than the white variety.

Shiitake Mushrooms

What they add: With their strong earthy fragrance and rich texture, shiitakes offer big flavor for few calories.

tempeh

The flavor of tempeh is stronger than tofu, but it still works well with a multitude of flavors and ethnic cuisines.

{ vegan recipe }
Tempeh Rendang

6 red Thai chiles
Cooking spray
1 cup minced shallots (about 6)
1½ tablespoons grated peeled fresh galangal
1 tablespoon grated peeled fresh ginger
1 tablespoon finely chopped peeled fresh
  lemongrass (about 1 stalk)
¼ teaspoon ground turmeric
1 cup light coconut milk
½ cup water
⅓ cup shredded unsweetened coconut, toasted
  and divided
1 teaspoon kosher salt
2 kaffir lime leaves
1½ pounds tempeh, cut into ½-inch cubes
2 tablespoons chopped fresh cilantro

1. Seed 5 chiles; leave seeds in 1 chile. Thinly slice chiles.
2. Heat a large nonstick skillet over medium heat; coat pan with cooking spray. Add chiles, shallots, and next 4 ingredients to pan; cook 5 minutes or until fragrant, stirring frequently. Add coconut milk, ½ cup water, 3 tablespoons coconut, salt, lime leaves, and tempeh to pan. Cover, reduce heat, and simmer 20 minutes or until sauce thickens. Discard lime leaves. Sprinkle with remaining 2 tablespoons coconut and cilantro. **Yield: 6 servings (serving size: 1 cup tempeh, 1 teaspoon coconut, and 1 teaspoon cilantro).**

CALORIES 353; FAT 13.9g (sat 5.8g, mono 3.1g, poly 2.2g); PROTEIN 28.4g; CARB 36.5g; FIBER 10.7g; CHOL 0mg; IRON 4.8mg; SODIUM 332mg; CALC 47mg

kitchen how-to: prepare lemongrass

This reedlike herb is accurately named. It looks like a long, grassy stalk and has a sweet lemon flavor and aroma. Because you only use the inner white portion of the stalk for cooking, you must remove the tough outer layers first.

1. Using a chef's knife, cut 1 inch from the root end, or base, of the lemongrass stalk.
2. Peel away and discard the tough, grassy outer layers until you reach the tender white inner portion.
3. Cut a section large enough to fit your needs, and use the side of your knife to crush the portion you've cut, just as you would garlic.
4. Add the crushed lemongrass to broths, stir-fries, or rice to impart lemon flavor; remove the crushed lemongrass before serving the dish. Or mince the lemongrass to add a subtle, lemony flavor to soups or stews; it's not necessary to remove minced lemongrass.

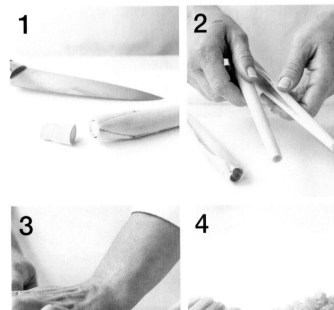

{ vegan recipe }
Tempeh Coconut Curry

- 1 tablespoon canola oil
- 2 cups finely chopped onion
- 1 teaspoon salt, divided
- 2 teaspoons tamarind pulp
- 1 tablespoon finely chopped peeled fresh ginger
- 1 tablespoon finely chopped fresh garlic
- 1½ teaspoons ground coriander
- ½ teaspoon ground turmeric
- ½ teaspoon crushed red pepper
- 1 (3-inch) cinnamon stick
- 3 cups chopped peeled sweet potato (about 1 pound)
- 1 cup water
- 1 (13.5-ounce) can light coconut milk
- 8 ounces organic tempeh, cut into ¾-inch cubes
- 1 tablespoon fresh lime juice
- 2 teaspoons less-sodium soy sauce
- 1½ cups uncooked basmati rice
- ⅓ cup chopped fresh cilantro
- ¼ teaspoon salt

1. To prepare curry, heat oil in a large nonstick skillet over medium-high heat. Add onion and ½ teaspoon salt. Cook 2 minutes or until onion is tender, stirring occasionally. Stir in tamarind; cook 2 minutes, stirring to break up tamarind. Add ginger and next 5 ingredients; cook 2 minutes, stirring frequently. Add remaining ½ teaspoon salt, potato, water, coconut milk, and tempeh; bring to a boil. Cover, reduce heat, and simmer 15 minutes or until potatoes are tender. Uncover; stir in juice and soy sauce. Simmer 3 minutes or until slightly thickened. Discard cinnamon stick.

2. To prepare rice, cook rice according to package instructions, omitting salt and fat. Stir in cilantro and ¼ teaspoon salt. Serve with curry. **Yield: 4 servings (serving size: 1 cup curry and about 1 cup rice).**

CALORIES 381; FAT 11.5g (sat 5.5g, mono 3.2g, poly 2.2g); PROTEIN 16.9g; CARB 53.7g; FIBER 6.3g; CHOL 0mg; IRON 2.9mg; SODIUM 870mg; CALC 112mg

Basmati Rice
What it adds: This aromatic, long-grain rice is dry and fluffy when cooked, which makes it a nice accompaniment to this fragrant curry.

Tamarind Pulp

What it adds: Tamarind, a common ingredient in Indian, Thai, and Mexican cuisines, adds an acidic, slightly tart flavor to food.

Light Coconut Milk

What it adds: While light coconut milk isn't as thick as the full-fat variety, the perk is that it contains 60 percent less fat.

Tempeh with Curried Cashew Sauce

Tempeh:
  2 tablespoons rice vinegar
  2 tablespoons less-sodium soy sauce
1½ tablespoons honey
1½ teaspoons finely chopped peeled fresh ginger
  1 garlic clove, minced
  1 (8-ounce) package organic tempeh, cut into
    ½-inch cubes

Sauce:
  1 teaspoon olive oil
  2 tablespoons coarsely chopped unsalted cashews
  ½ cup chopped onion
  ½ teaspoon curry powder
  1 garlic clove, minced
  ¼ cup 2% reduced-fat milk
  2 tablespoons hot water
  ⅛ teaspoon salt

Remaining Ingredients:
  Coarsely chopped unsalted cashews (optional)
  Chopped fresh parsley (optional)
  1 (6-inch) whole-wheat pita, cut into 4 wedges

1. To prepare tempeh, heat a medium saucepan over medium-high heat. Add first 5 ingredients to pan, stirring with a whisk. Add tempeh; bring to a boil. Cook 3 minutes or until liquid is almost evaporated, stirring frequently. Place tempeh mixture in a medium bowl; cover and keep warm.

2. To prepare sauce, heat oil in a small saucepan over medium-high heat. Add cashews to pan, and cook 2 minutes or until lightly browned. Add onion to pan; sauté 3 minutes or until tender. Add curry powder and 1 garlic clove to pan; cook 1 minute, stirring constantly. Remove from heat. Stir in milk.

3. Place cashew mixture, 2 tablespoons hot water, and salt in a blender. Remove center piece of blender lid (to allow steam to escape); secure blender lid on blender. Place a clean towel over opening in blender lid (to avoid splatters). Blend until smooth, scraping sides. Add cashew sauce to tempeh in bowl; toss gently to coat. Garnish with chopped cashews and chopped parsley, if you'd like. Serve with pita wedges. **Yield: 2 servings (serving size: about 1 cup tempeh mixture and 2 pita wedges).**

CALORIES 414; FAT 12.9g (sat 3.5g, mono 4.2g, poly 1g); PROTEIN 30.7g; CARB 48.2g; FIBER 9.6g; CHOL 2mg; IRON 5.3mg; SODIUM 778mg; CALC 248mg

kitchen how-to:
peel & grate fresh ginger

The papery brown skin and gnarled root of fresh ginger can be puzzling to deal with if you are unfamiliar with it. Its powerful scent and peppery flavor smooth out during cooking and add a liveliness to dishes.

1. Use a vegetable peeler to remove the tough skin and reveal the flesh.

2. To grate ginger, rub a peeled piece of ginger across a fine grater such as a microplane.

{ vegan recipe }
Vegetable Tagine with Baked Tempeh

Tagine:
- 1 teaspoon cumin seeds
- 1 teaspoon caraway seeds
- 1 teaspoon coriander seeds
- ½ teaspoon paprika
- ½ teaspoon black peppercorns
- 1 (1-inch) piece cinnamon stick
- 2 teaspoons extra-virgin olive oil
- 2 cups finely chopped onion
- ¾ cup finely chopped carrot
- ½ cup finely chopped celery
- ½ teaspoon sea salt
- 2 garlic cloves, peeled
- 2 cups (½-inch) cubed peeled sweet potato
- 2 cups chopped green cabbage
- 1½ cups water
- 1 cup finely chopped yellow squash
- 1 cup finely chopped zucchini
- 1 cup finely chopped peeled tomato
- 1 tablespoon fresh lemon juice

Tempeh:
- ⅔ cup water
- 6 tablespoons fresh lemon juice
- ⅓ cup finely chopped fresh flat-leaf parsley
- 2 teaspoons ground cumin
- 2 teaspoons paprika
- ½ teaspoon sea salt
- ½ teaspoon ground red pepper
- 4 garlic cloves, minced
- 1 pound tempeh, cut into ½-inch cubes

Remaining Ingredients:
- 2 cups hot cooked couscous
- 4 teaspoons minced fresh cilantro (optional)

1. To prepare tagine, combine first 6 ingredients in a spice or coffee grinder; process until finely ground.
2. Heat oil in a large Dutch oven over medium heat. Add onion, carrot, celery, ½ teaspoon salt, and 2 peeled garlic cloves; cook 5 minutes, stirring occasionally. Cover, reduce heat to low, and cook 20 minutes.
3. Stir in cumin mixture, sweet potato, and next 5 ingredients; bring to a boil. Reduce heat; simmer, uncovered, 30 minutes or until thick. Stir in lemon juice.
4. To prepare tempeh, preheat oven to 350°.
5. Combine ⅔ cup water and next 7 ingredients in a large bowl. Add tempeh, and toss well to coat. Arrange the tempeh mixture in a single layer in an 11 x 7–inch baking dish. Cover with foil.
6. Bake at 350° for 35 minutes. Uncover and bake an additional 5 minutes or until liquid is absorbed. Serve tempeh over tagine and couscous; sprinkle with cilantro, if desired. **Yield: 4 servings (serving size: 4 ounces tempeh, ¾ cup tagine, and ½ cup couscous).**

CALORIES 507; FAT 16.1g (sat 3g, mono 5.3g, poly 5.1g); PROTEIN 29.5g; CARB 69.3g; FIBER 16.3g; CHOL 0mg; IRON 6.4mg; SODIUM 642mg; CALC 262mg

kitchen how-to:
peel & seed a tomato

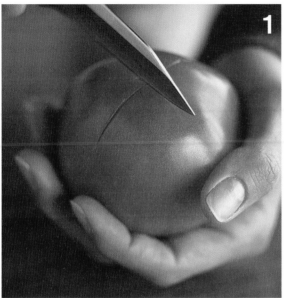

No matter what time of year, store tomatoes at room temperature out of direct sunlight. Above all, to preserve flavor and texture, keep the tomatoes out of the refrigerator.

1. Using a sharp knife, cut a shallow "X" in the bottom of each tomato.

2. Drop the tomatoes into boiling water for 15 to 20 seconds; remove them with a slotted spoon or tongs.

3. Plunge the tomatoes into ice water; remove and discard the skins.

4. Using a small paring knife, cut a small circle around the stem end of the tomato. With the tip of the knife, remove the core.

5. Cut the tomatoes in half horizontally. Cup each tomato half in the palm of your hand, cut side up; gently squeeze out the seeds. You can also scoop out the seeds with your fingers.

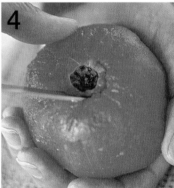

{vegan recipe}
Tempeh Ratatouille

We swapped tempeh for traditional eggplant in this ratatouille. You can use any fresh vegetable combination in this easy sauté.

1 teaspoon extra-virgin olive oil
8 ounces organic tempeh, cut into ½-inch cubes
Cooking spray
1 cup finely chopped onion (about 1 large)
¾ teaspoon kosher salt
¼ teaspoon crushed red pepper
2 garlic cloves, minced
½ cup organic vegetable broth
1 cup yellow squash (about ½ pound), cut into 1-inch cubes
1 cup zucchini (about ½ pound), cut into ½-inch cubes
1 (8-ounce) package mushrooms, halved
1 cup halved cherry tomatoes
½ cup (½-inch) pieces red bell pepper (about ½ large pepper)
2 tablespoons chopped fresh basil
1 tablespoon chopped fresh flat-leaf parsley
1 teaspoon fresh lemon juice

1. Preheat oven to 500°.
2. Combine oil and tempeh in a baking pan coated with cooking spray, tossing to coat tempeh. Bake at 500° for 10 minutes or until tempeh is browned on the edges, stirring once.
3. Heat a large nonstick skillet over medium-high heat; coat pan with cooking spray. Add onion; sauté 3 minutes or until browned. Stir in salt, crushed red pepper, and garlic; sauté 30 seconds. Add broth; bring to a boil. Stir in tempeh, squash, zucchini, and mushrooms; simmer 5 minutes. Stir in tomatoes and bell pepper; simmer 5 minutes. Remove from heat; stir in basil, parsley, and juice. **Yield: 4 servings (serving size: 1 cup).**

CALORIES 163; FAT 4.7g (sat 1.3g, mono 1.8g, poly 1.4g); PROTEIN 16.3g; CARB 17.2g; FIBER 6.3g; CHOL 0mg; IRON 2.8mg; SODIUM 440mg; CALC 132mg

kitchen how-to:
easily cube zucchini & squash

To quickly cube zucchini and squash, cut each vegetable lengthwise into slices. Stack the slices, and cut them lengthwise again into strips. Then, keeping the strips piled together, cut them crosswise into cubes.

{vegan recipe}
Tempeh and Wild Mushroom Fricassee

Cooking spray

12 ounces tempeh, cut into ½-inch cubes

¼ cup dry white wine

2 tablespoons less-sodium soy sauce

4 cups thinly sliced leeks (about 4 large)

2 cups sliced button mushrooms

2 cups sliced cremini mushrooms

2 cups diced shiitake mushroom caps (about 4 ounces)

2 (4-inch) portobello mushroom caps, gills removed, chopped

1 tablespoon all-purpose flour

⅓ cup celery leaves

2 thyme sprigs

1 parsley sprig

½ cup thinly sliced garlic (about 20 cloves)

1 (14½-ounce) can organic vegetable broth (such as Swanson Certified Organic)

1 tablespoon fresh lemon juice

¼ teaspoon fine sea salt

¼ teaspoon freshly ground black pepper

2 tablespoons chopped fresh parsley

1 tablespoon grated lemon rind (optional)

1. Heat a Dutch oven coated with cooking spray over medium-high heat. Add tempeh; sauté 8 minutes or until golden brown. Add wine and soy sauce; cook 15 seconds or until liquid almost evaporates. Remove tempeh from pan.

2. Add leeks and mushrooms to pan; sauté 5 minutes. Stir in flour; cook 1 minute, stirring frequently. Tie celery leaves, thyme sprigs, and parsley sprig together securely with string. Add herbs, garlic, and broth to pan; bring to a boil. Add tempeh, stirring well. Cover, reduce heat, and simmer 15 minutes.

3. Uncover and cook 3 minutes or until thick. Discard herbs. Stir in lemon juice, salt, and pepper; sprinkle with parsley. Garnish each serving with ½ teaspoon lemon rind, if desired. **Yield: 6 servings (serving size: 1 cup).**

CALORIES 317; FAT 10.4g (sat 2g, mono 2.6g, poly 3.6g); PROTEIN 23.7g; CARB 37.8g; FIBER 8.6g; CHOL 0mg; IRON 6.2mg; SODIUM 898mg; CALC 206mg

kitchen how-to: wash leeks

Notorious for hiding dirt within their concentric layers, leeks require thorough washing. We show you another way to wash leeks on page 375.

1. To clean, trim the roots with a sharp knife.
2. Remove the dark green leaves at the opposite end of the leek, cutting at the point where the color changes from light to dark; halve it lengthwise. If a recipe calls for sliced or chopped leeks, cut them first, and place the pieces in a bowl of cold water; agitate gently, allowing any debris to fall to the bottom. Use a strainer to carefully remove the leeks from the bowl. Repeat as necessary, and then rinse in a colander. If a recipe calls for halved leeks, hold the leek halves with the white tops pointing up, and gently fan the layers under running water. This allows the grit to wash away with the water.

way to cook vegetarian
salads

salads

Salads are a great vegetarian option. They're easy to make, infinitely variable, and seasonally adjustable—and they're a great way to sample an array of fruits and vegetables. Variety is key: You want to benefit from the huge number of healthful compounds in different plants. Variety also helps prevent salad fatigue.

Whole-Grain Salads

Salads are a clever way to work more whole grains into your diet and reap all their nutritional benefits—they're loaded with fiber, which helps you maintain a healthy weight, keeps your heart healthy, and aids in digestion. They're also a great vegetable source of protein.

Hearty whole grains, which offer a pleasantly chewy texture when they're cooked, include farro and wheat berries (hard winter wheat). Cook them according to the package directions, and toss them with your favorite chopped fresh herbs and a tangy vinaigrette. Fresh chopped raw vegetables, such as radish or carrot, add additional crunch; you can also roast winter squash or root vegetables and toss them with farro or wheat berries. Adding shaved or crumbled cheese gives rich, creamy contrast.

More familiar whole grains, such as pearled barley, bulgur, and quinoa, also make a versatile base for salads. Since these grains absorb excess liquid, add small amounts of a sharp dressing, such as a vinaigrette—thick, creamy dressings may be too heavy for them. Add chopped raw vegetables and toasted nuts or seeds for texture. See page 14 for more information about whole grains.

Pick the Perfect Greens When you make a tossed salad, first choose the lettuce or salad greens you'll use. Many choices are available, so it helps to know what flavor and texture to expect and what type of dressing works best with the different kinds of greens. Most lettuces or salad greens fall into a few broad categories.

Peppery Greens: This category includes arugula (above, top right) and watercress (above, left). These lettuces pack a spicy punch, so they can stand up to other strong flavors. These lettuces are also great mixed in with milder lettuces.

Hearty Lettuces: Lettuces such as romaine (above, top) and iceberg (above, bottom) are good choices for heavier, thick and creamy dressings, such as Caesar and blue cheese.

Mild Lettuces: These lettuces include (clockwise from top) butter lettuces, such as Boston and Bibb, as well as spinach, leafy green and red lettuce, and mâche. All of these are mild in flavor and tend to be delicate, so pair them with tart vinaigrettes and other assertive flavors.

Bitter Greens: This group includes (clockwise from top right) radicchio (even though it's a vibrant red color), escarole, endive, and frisée. These lettuces have a pleasantly bitter flavor. Pair them with fatty ingredients, such as nuts, olives, and good-quality oil, or sweet ingredients, such as fruits. The fat and sweetness balance the bitterness of the greens.

{ vegan recipe }

Watercress, Frisée, and Grapefruit Salad with Curry Vinaigrette

- 4 cups trimmed watercress (about 1 bunch)
- 4 cups torn frisée (about 1 head)
- 1 cup red grapefruit sections (about 2 grapefruit)
- 1 cup thinly sliced red onion
- 8 whole pitted dates, sliced
- 2 tablespoons white balsamic vinegar
- ½ teaspoon curry powder
- ½ teaspoon salt
- 5 teaspoons grapeseed oil

1. Arrange watercress and frisée on a large platter, and top evenly with grapefruit, onion, and dates.
2. Combine vinegar, curry powder, and salt in a small bowl, and slowly add oil, stirring constantly with a whisk. Drizzle over salad. Serve immediately. **Yield: 8 servings (serving size: about 1 cup).**

CALORIES 79; FAT 3g (sat 0.3g, mono 0.5g, poly 2g); PROTEIN 1.4g; CARB 13.5g; FIBER 2.3g; CHOL 0mg; IRON 0.4mg; SODIUM 162mg; CALC 46mg

kitchen how-to:
section grapefruit

To section grapefruit, trim away the peel and bitter white pith; then use a sharp paring knife to cut the sections between the membranes.

Grapeseed Oil
What it adds: Grapeseed oil provides healthy fats and vitamin E. It has a mild flavor. You can substitute canola oil, if you prefer.

Dates
What they add: Sugary dates provide a sweet contrast to the salad's bitter greens.

Raspberries
What they add: These berries add bright color and good-for-you nutrients like fiber, antioxidants, and vitamin C.

Chives
What they add: Members of the onion family, chives not only add great flavor to this salad, but they also provide phenols and flavonoids.

kitchen how-to: roast beets

Roasting beets concentrates their natural sugars and intensifies their flavor.

1. Using a sharp knife, trim the beets, leaving the root and 1 inch of the stem on each beet. Scrub each beet with a vegetable brush. Place the beets on a foil-lined jelly-roll pan coated with cooking spray. Lightly coat the beets with cooking spray.

2. Bake at 400° for 45 minutes or until tender. Cool the beets slightly. Trim off about ¼ inch of the beet roots.

3. Rub off the skins. They should slip off easily after cooking.

{ vegan recipe }

Middle Eastern Eggplant Salad

Reminiscent of baba ghanoush, this salad can be served as a dip with crackers or flatbread.

2 medium red bell peppers
1 medium tomato, peeled and seeded
3 tablespoons no-salt-added tomato
   paste
2 tablespoons water
½ teaspoon salt, divided
Dash of ground red pepper
3 garlic cloves, thinly sliced
¼ cup olive oil
1 pound eggplant, cut into (1-inch)
   cubes
¼ teaspoon freshly ground black
   pepper

1. Preheat broiler.
2. Cut bell peppers in half lengthwise; discard seeds and membranes. Place pepper halves, skin sides up, on a foil-lined baking sheet; flatten with hand. Broil 12 minutes or until blackened. Place in a zip-top plastic bag; seal. Let stand 10 minutes. Peel and chop.
3. Place tomato in a blender; process until smooth. Add tomato paste, 2 tablespoons water, ¼ teaspoon salt, ground red pepper, and garlic to the blender; process until smooth.
4. Heat oil in a saucepan over medium heat. Add eggplant; cook 30 minutes or until tender, stirring frequently. Stir in bell pepper and tomato mixture. Cook 5 minutes. Stir in remaining ¼ teaspoon salt and black pepper.
Yield: 4 servings (serving size: ½ cup).

CALORIES 182; FAT 14.1g (sat 2g, mono 9.9g, poly 1.7g); PROTEIN 2.7g; CARB 14.6g; FIBER 6g; CHOL 0.3mg; IRON 1.2mg; SODIUM 315mg; CALC 25mg

kitchen how-to: cube eggplant

Fresh eggplant, which can be found in supermarkets from June through September, has a sparkling jewel-like color with shiny, smooth skin. It should feel heavy in your hand and be firm but slightly springy. The skin is edible, so you can simply cut the eggplant into 1-inch slices (or whatever size you need), and then cut each slice into cubes.

Stacked Heirloom Tomato Salad with Ricotta Salata Cream

Use a variety of heirloom tomato colors for the prettiest presentation. Unlike ricotta cheese, ricotta salata is firm enough to crumble or grate; you can substitute feta cheese for ricotta salata, if you prefer.

6 (1-ounce) slices country peasant loaf bread
Cooking spray
1 garlic clove, halved
½ cup (2 ounces) crumbled ricotta salata cheese
½ cup (4 ounces) reduced-fat silken tofu
2 tablespoons water
2 tablespoons fresh lemon juice
1 garlic clove, minced
6 medium tomatoes, cut into ⅓-inch-thick slices (about 3¼ pounds)
¼ cup thinly sliced fresh basil
1 teaspoon coarsely ground black pepper

1. Prepare grill or grill pan.
2. Place bread on grill rack or grill pan coated with cooking spray; grill 2 minutes on each side or until lightly browned. Remove from grill. Rub cut sides of halved garlic clove over one side of each bread slice. Set aside.
3. Combine cheese, tofu, water, lemon juice, and minced garlic in a blender; process until smooth.
4. Place one bread slice on each of 6 plates; divide tomato slices evenly among servings. Spoon about 1 tablespoon cheese mixture on each serving; sprinkle evenly with basil and pepper. **Yield: 6 servings.**

CALORIES 168; FAT 4.9g (sat 2.3g, mono 1.8g, poly 0.6g); PROTEIN 7.6g; CARB 26.7g; FIBER 3.7g; CHOL 10mg; IRON 2mg; SODIUM 339mg; CALC 49mg

all about heirloom tomatoes

Heirloom tomatoes have become increasingly popular and easy to find in summer months. They range in color from yellow to purple, and in form from grape-size to sausage-shaped and heavy, fat globes. In general, yellow and orange tomatoes are lower in acidity and thus taste sweeter than the more tart red or green varieties. Purple varieties have a deep, complex flavor similar to that of red wine.

kitchen how-to: prepare garlic bread

Rubbing toasted bread with halved garlic cloves is the traditional way to make garlic bread, and the cloves lend a better, fresher garlic flavor than garlic powder.

Kiwifruit
What it adds: The kiwifruit adds a beautiful green to this colorful salad. Try using golden kiwifruit instead for a sweeter taste and pretty golden color.

Honeydew
What it adds: Ripe honeydew adds a light and fresh taste to the salad.

{ vegan recipe }
Radish Slaw with New York Deli Dressing

In this colorful slaw, peppery radishes stand in for cabbage. The vinegar-based dressing gets a big flavor boost from mustard oil; its pungent bite enhances the radish flavor. It's worth seeking out—look for it with other specialty oils at your supermarket.

- 4 **cups shredded radishes (about 40 radishes)**
- 2 **cups finely chopped yellow bell pepper**
- 1½ **cups shredded carrot**
- ½ **cup white wine vinegar**
- 4 **teaspoons sugar**
- 1 **tablespoon chopped fresh dill**
- 1 **tablespoon mustard oil or olive oil**
- ½ **teaspoon salt**
- ½ **teaspoon black pepper**

1. Combine first 3 ingredients in a large bowl. Combine white wine vinegar and remaining ingredients, stirring with a whisk. Drizzle dressing over slaw; toss well to combine. Serve immediately. **Yield: 10 servings (serving size: ¾ cup).**

CALORIES 46; FAT 1.8g (sat 0.2g, mono 0.9g, poly 0.4g); PROTEIN 0.9g; CARB 7.4g; FIBER 1.6g; CHOL 0mg; IRON 0.5mg; SODIUM 136mg; CALC 20mg

kitchen how-to:
shred radishes

Use a shredding blade in a food processor for easier preparation. Place the radishes in a food processor (you may have to do this in batches depending on the number of radishes you're shredding and the size of your food processor); process until shredded.

all about buying radishes

Whether you're shopping for humble red radishes or exotic heirloom varieties, look for ones that are small for their type with smooth surfaces and bright, intact greens.

{ vegan recipe }
Fennel Slaw with Orange Vinaigrette

Use a mandoline to cut the fennel into thin, uniform slices.

- ¼ cup extra-virgin olive oil
- 1 tablespoon sherry vinegar
- 1 teaspoon grated orange rind
- 1½ tablespoons fresh orange juice
- 1 teaspoon kosher salt
- ¼ teaspoon freshly ground black pepper
- ¼ teaspoon crushed red pepper
- 3 medium fennel bulbs with stalks (about 4 pounds)
- 2 cups orange sections (about 2 large oranges)
- ½ cup coarsely chopped pitted green olives

1. Combine first 7 ingredients in a large bowl.
2. Trim tough outer leaves from fennel; mince feathery fronds to measure 1 cup. Remove and discard stalks. Cut fennel bulb in half lengthwise; discard core. Thinly slice bulbs. Add fronds, fennel slices, and orange sections to bowl; toss gently to combine. Sprinkle with olives. **Yield: 16 servings (serving size: ¾ cup).**

CALORIES 64; FAT 4.4g (sat 0.5g, mono 3.1g, poly 0.7g); PROTEIN 0.8g; CARB 6.5g; FIBER 1.9g; CHOL 0mg; IRON 0.4mg; SODIUM 230mg; CALC 31mg

kitchen how-to:
easily juice an orange

There are plenty of ways to get fresh juice from citrus using a variety of gadgets—a wooden reamer, saucer juicer, and countertop juicer. But the simplest way that requires no special equipment is to cut the orange in half, insert a fork, and, holding the orange over a bowl, squeeze the fruit against the tines.

all about buying oranges

Choose firm oranges that have smooth skins and are not moldy. Don't worry about brown patches on the skin; they don't indicate poor quality. You can store oranges at room temperature for up to one week or in the refrigerator for up to three weeks.

{ vegan recipe }

Light and Fresh Potato Salad

Dressing:
- ¼ cup seasoned rice vinegar
- 2 tablespoons canola oil
- ¼ teaspoon salt
- ⅛ teaspoon freshly ground black pepper

Salad:
- 5 cups cubed red potato (about 2 pounds)
- ½ teaspoon salt
- 1 cup chopped peeled cucumber
- ¾ cup sliced grape or cherry tomatoes
- ¾ cup chopped green bell pepper
- ½ cup chopped orange bell pepper
- ¼ cup chopped green onions
- 1 (2¼-ounce) can sliced ripe olives, drained

1. To prepare dressing, combine first 4 ingredients in a large bowl; stir with a whisk.

2. To prepare salad, place potato and ½ teaspoon salt in a medium saucepan. Cover with water to 2 inches above potato; bring to a boil. Reduce heat, and simmer 8 minutes or until tender; drain.

3. Add potato to dressing in bowl, tossing gently to coat; let stand 15 minutes. Stir in cucumber and remaining ingredients; toss well. Cover and chill.

Yield: 12 servings (serving size: ¾ cup).

CALORIES 90; FAT 2.8g (sat 0.2g, mono 1.6g, poly 0.8g); PROTEIN 1.8g; CARB 14.9g; FIBER 2g; CHOL 0mg; IRON 0.9mg; SODIUM 295mg; CALC 19mg

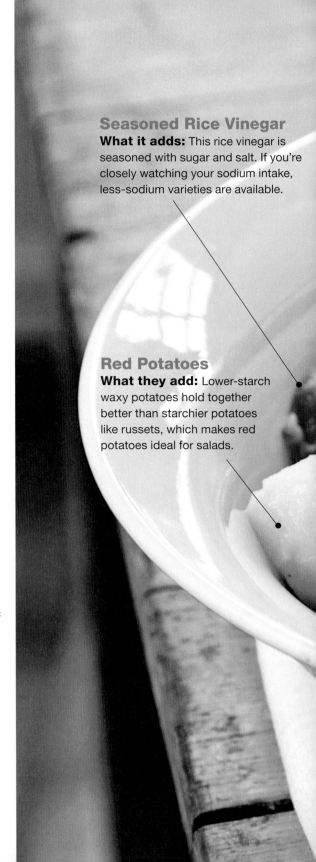

Seasoned Rice Vinegar
What it adds: This rice vinegar is seasoned with sugar and salt. If you're closely watching your sodium intake, less-sodium varieties are available.

Red Potatoes
What they add: Lower-starch waxy potatoes hold together better than starchier potatoes like russets, which makes red potatoes ideal for salads.

Black Olives

What they add: Olives are a source of good-for-you monounsaturated fats and vitamin E.

Fresh Oregano
What it adds: This Mediterranean-style salad highlights the pungent, slightly peppery tang of oregano. Oregano's milder cousin, marjoram, would make a good substitute.

{ vegan recipe }
Minty Bulgur Wheat and Peach Salad

- 2 **cups boiling water**
- 1 **cup uncooked bulgur wheat**
- 3 **tablespoons fresh lemon juice**
- 2 **tablespoons fresh lime juice**
- 2 **tablespoons extra-virgin olive oil**
- 1 **tablespoon honey**
- ½ **teaspoon salt**
- ¼ **teaspoon freshly ground black pepper**
- 2 **cups diced, peeled peach (about 2 medium)**
- 2 **cups diced, peeled jicama**
- 1 **cup finely chopped fresh mint**

1. Combine boiling water and bulgur in a large bowl; let stand 1 hour or until water is absorbed. Combine juices and next 4 ingredients, stirring well with a whisk. Add peach, jicama, and mint to bulgur; toss to combine. Drizzle dressing mixture over bulgur mixture; toss to coat. Chill 1 hour. **Yield: 8 servings (serving size: about 1 cup).**

CALORIES 162; FAT 5.7g (sat 0.8g, mono 3.7g, poly 0.7g); PROTEIN 3.3g; CARB 27.6g; FIBER 6.6g; CHOL 0mg; IRON 2.2mg; SODIUM 156mg; CALC 34mg

kitchen how-to:
peel & dice jicama

Delicious raw and cooked, this sweet, nutty root adds a cool crunch to salads and stir-fries. Jicama (HEE-kah-ma) has thin brown skin and crisp, juicy, white flesh that's mild in flavor (think of a cross between a water chestnut and a pear). You can find jicama year-round in the produce section of many supermarkets and Latin American markets. Select firm, dry jicama roots; the skin should not appear shriveled, bruised, or blemished.

1. Using a vegetable peeler, remove the skin.
2. Once peeled, cut the jicama into slices. Stack the slices, and then cut them into strips. Cut across the strips. You can use this same method if your recipe calls for cubes or thin strips.

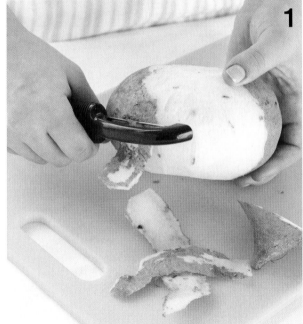

1

2

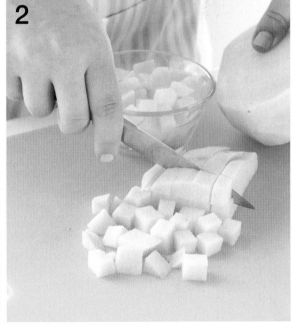

{ vegan recipe }

Quinoa and Pistachio Salad with Moroccan Pesto

1 red bell pepper
1 cup uncooked quinoa
1 cup organic vegetable broth
½ cup water
½ cup fresh orange juice
⅓ cup coarsely chopped fresh cilantro
¼ cup extra-virgin olive oil
2 tablespoons coarsely chopped fresh flat-leaf parsley
3 tablespoons fresh lemon juice
½ teaspoon ground cumin
¼ teaspoon kosher salt
¼ teaspoon ground red pepper
2 large garlic cloves, coarsely chopped
1 (15.5-ounce) can chickpeas (garbanzo beans), rinsed and drained
12 oil-cured olives, pitted and chopped
¼ cup chopped pistachios

1. Preheat broiler.
2. Cut red bell pepper in half lengthwise; discard seeds and membranes. Place pepper halves, skin sides up, on a foil-lined baking sheet; flatten with hand. Broil 12 minutes or until blackened. Place in a zip-top plastic bag; seal. Let stand 10 minutes. Peel and chop.
3. Place quinoa, broth, ½ cup water, and juice in a large saucepan; bring to a boil. Cover, reduce heat, and simmer 12 minutes or until liquid is absorbed.
4. Place cilantro and next 7 ingredients in a food processor; process until smooth. Combine bell pepper, quinoa mixture, cilantro mixture, chickpeas, and olives in a large bowl. Sprinkle with nuts. **Yield: 6 servings (serving size: ¾ cup).**

CALORIES 322; FAT 16.6g (sat 2.2g, mono 10.9g, poly 2.7g); PROTEIN 7.8g; CARB 37.3g; FIBER 5.2g; CHOL 0mg; IRON 4.1mg; SODIUM 344mg; CALC 55mg

kitchen how-to: prepare quinoa

Quinoa is a quick-cooking whole grain that supplies protein, iron, and vitamin E.

1. Place the uncooked quinoa and water (or combination of liquids, such as broth, juice, and water) in a large saucepan. You'll need 2 cups of liquid for every cup of uncooked quinoa you're preparing.
2. Bring to a boil. Cover, reduce the heat, and simmer the quinoa mixture 12 minutes or until the liquid is absorbed.

Spelt Salad with White Beans and Artichokes

1¼ cups uncooked spelt, rinsed and drained
2½ cups water
⅓ cup chopped fresh mint
⅓ cup chopped fresh parsley
¼ cup minced red onion
3 tablespoons fresh lemon juice
2 tablespoons olive oil
¼ teaspoon salt
⅛ teaspoon freshly ground black pepper
1 (15-ounce) can navy beans, rinsed and drained
1 (14-ounce) can artichoke hearts, drained
and chopped

1. Combine spelt and 2½ cups water in a medium saucepan; bring to a boil. Cover, reduce heat, and simmer 30 minutes or until tender and liquid is absorbed.

2. Combine cooked spelt, mint, and remaining ingredients in a large bowl, stirring well. Cover and store in the refrigerator. **Yield: 5 servings (serving size: 1 cup).**

CALORIES 204; FAT 6.5g (sat 0.8g, mono 4g, poly 0.9g); PROTEIN 7.4g; CARB 30.7g; FIBER 4.9g; CHOL 0mg; IRON 3.2mg; SODIUM 437mg; CALC 40mg

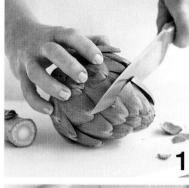

1

kitchen how-to:
reach the heart of an artichoke

You can substitute fresh artichokes for canned, if you'd like. Fresh artichokes have a denser, richer flavor when compared to canned (and less sodium). Prepping an artichoke takes a little bit of time, but once you discard the inedible "choke," this thistle's nutty flavor jazzes up a variety of dishes, including pizza, and it makes a great appetizer. Plus, artichokes contain potassium, vitamin A, and antioxidants. Baby artichokes are entirely edible, even the choke. To prepare an artichoke, trim away the stem, top portion, and outer leaves as described below, and then cook it.

1. Cut the stem so the artichoke sits on its base without wobbling. Slice off a quarter of the artichoke's top.
2. Pull away the outside leaves until you reach the yellow center.

3. Cut the artichoke in half lengthwise, and pull or cut out any purple, spiky leaves. You'll see a fuzzy area—that's the choke.
4. Using a sharp-edged spoon (such as a grapefruit spoon), scoop out the fuzzy choke until no hair fibers remain. Discard.
5. Turn over the artichoke, and peel away the tough green exterior at the base with a knife, as if you were peeling an apple. You'll soon reach the yellow flesh.
6. Rinse the artichoke in an acid bath of ¼ cup lemon juice mixed with 1 cup water. This helps stop the browning process, which occurs when the flesh comes into contact with air. Cook the artichoke as desired or steam it, keeping the artichoke covered, until it gives when poked at the base with a knife (just like testing a potato for doneness).

2

3

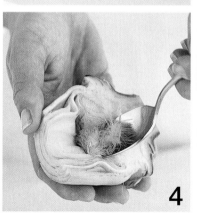

4

5

6

Wheat Berry Salad with Goat Cheese

Taking a cue from traditional tabbouleh, this dish uses lots of peak-season vegetables, tart lemon juice, and pungent fresh herbs. Serve it with toasted pita wedges.

1¼ cups wheat berries (hard winter wheat)
2½ cups chopped English cucumber
⅔ cup thinly sliced green onions
1½ cups loosely packed chopped arugula
6 tablespoons minced fresh flat-leaf parsley
1 pint grape tomatoes, halved
1 tablespoon grated lemon rind
3 tablespoons fresh lemon juice
1 teaspoon kosher salt
½ teaspoon freshly ground black pepper
½ teaspoon sugar
2 tablespoons extra-virgin olive oil
¾ cup (3 ounces) crumbled goat cheese

1. Place wheat berries in a medium bowl; cover with water to 2 inches above wheat berries. Cover and let stand 8 hours. Drain.
2. Place wheat berries in a medium saucepan; cover with water to 2 inches above wheat berries. Bring to a boil, reduce heat, and cook, uncovered, 1 hour or until tender. Drain and rinse with cold water; drain well. Place wheat berries in a large bowl; add cucumber and next 4 ingredients.
3. Combine rind and next 4 ingredients in a bowl; gradually add oil, stirring constantly with a whisk. Drizzle dressing over salad; toss well to coat. Stir in cheese. Let stand at least 30 minutes; serve at room temperature.
Yield: 6 servings (serving size: about 1⅓ cups).

CALORIES 253; FAT 9.7g (sat 3.7g, mono 4.4g, poly 0.9g); PROTEIN 9.2g; CARB 35.7g; FIBER 6.8g; CHOL 11mg; IRON 1.2mg; SODIUM 401mg; CALC 79mg

kitchen how-to:
prepare wheat berries

Wheat berries (hard winter wheat) have a chewy texture. They're simple to prepare, and they require little attention while cooking.

1. Place the wheat berries in a bowl, and cover with water to 2 inches above the wheat berries. Cover and let stand 8 hours. Drain.
2. Place wheat berries in a medium saucepan; cover with water 2 inches above wheat berries. Bring to a boil, reduce the heat, and cook, uncovered, 1 hour or until tender.

way to cook vegetarian
sandwiches

sandwiches

Whether you're looking for a grab-and-go lunch or a light supper, vegetarian sandwiches offer a quick-and-easy solution with endless variations and flavors.

Simple Sandwich Additions

The condiments and added extra toppings—tomatoes, cucumber, lettuce, olives—can often transform an average sandwich into something extraordinary. Here are some flavorful ingredients that can help make your next sandwich stellar.

Pesto: Even though it's made with high-calorie ingredients like nuts, olive oil, and cheese, pesto is a healthful spread. One tablespoon supplies a reasonable 58 calories and 5 grams of good-for-you unsaturated fat. Pesto perks up milder ingredients; try spreading it on your next sandwich.

Roasted Red Peppers: Red peppers are naturally sweet and roasting them adds a smoky, savory accent. You can buy bottled roasted red peppers at the supermarket, or you can roast your own (see page 24). Add them to a classic grilled cheese on whole-grain bread. Or line a flour tortilla with baby spinach and roasted bell peppers, sprinkle on diced garlic and basil feta cheese, and roll it up burrito-style.

Avocado: Avocados are high in fat, but 64 percent of it is heart-healthy monounsaturated fat. They also provide other nutrients like vitamin E and potassium. Try thin slivers of mild, buttery avocado on an English muffin filled with alfalfa sprouts, sliced radishes, and sharp cheese.

Pear: Pears make the perfect sandwich fruit because they add sweetness and crunch without overpowering other flavors. Add pears to a sandwich with Brie and mustard on whole-grain bread. Or sauté the pears to heighten their flavor even more, toss them with feta cheese and lemon vinaigrette, and serve the filling in a whole-grain pita.

Building Your Own Vegetable Burger

You can easily create a vegetable burger at home using beans, grains, and fresh vegetables—nutrient-packed ingredients that are high in protein and dietary fiber but low in saturated fat. Start with a protein source, such as beans or soy. Add a whole grain, such as oatmeal, or nuts for texture. Then build layers of flavor using fresh or sautéed vegetables, herbs, and spices. A binding agent like breadcrumbs holds the mixture together and absorbs excess moisture so you can form patties and cook the burgers on the grill or in a skillet with a small amount of oil.

kitchen how-to: make mayonnaise

Mayonnaise can be made into an almost infinite number of variations—curry, saffron or cooked mushroom. Just let your imagination be your guide.

1. The secret to success when making mayonnaise is to start the emulsion quickly. Using a combination of egg yolks and Dijon mustard is the key to a great finished mayonnaise. Combine 1 teaspoon fresh lemon juice, ½ teaspoon Dijon mustard, and 2 large pasteurized egg yolks in a medium bowl, stirring well with a whisk.

2. The mayonnaise will thicken as you begin to incorporate more oil. Gradually add ¾ cup of canola oil to the egg yolk mixture, at first just adding it drop by drop, stirring with a whisk until each addition is incorporated. Once the emulsion is formed, add the oil about 1 tablespoon at a time, and continue stirring constantly until the mixture is thick. **Yield: about 1 cup (serving size: about 1 tablespoon).**

CALORIES 100; FAT 11.1g (sat 0.9g, mono 6.4g, poly 3.2g); PROTEIN 0.3g; CARB 0.1g; FIBER 0g; CHOL 26mg; IRON 0.1mg; SODIUM 2mg; CALC 3mg

Baked Falafel Sandwiches with Yogurt-Tahini Sauce

It's worth the effort to seek out thick, rich, creamy Greek yogurt. Make the sauce up to three days in advance and the falafel mixture up to one day ahead; bake the falafel patties just before you serve them.

Sauce:
- 1 cup plain whole-milk Greek yogurt (such as Fage Total Classic)
- 1 tablespoon tahini (sesame-seed paste)
- 1 tablespoon fresh lemon juice

Falafel:
- ¾ cup water
- ¼ cup uncooked bulgur
- 2 (15.5-ounce) cans chickpeas (garbanzo beans), rinsed and drained

- 3 cups cooked chickpeas (garbanzo beans)
- ½ cup chopped fresh cilantro
- ½ cup chopped green onions
- ⅓ to ½ cup water
- 2 tablespoons all-purpose flour
- 1 tablespoon ground cumin
- 1 teaspoon baking powder
- ¾ teaspoon salt
- ¼ to ½ teaspoon ground red pepper
- 3 garlic cloves
- Cooking spray

Remaining Ingredients:
- 6 (2.8-ounce) Mediterranean Style white flatbreads (such as Toufayan)
- 12 (¼-inch-thick) slices tomato
- Chopped fresh cilantro (optional)

1. To prepare sauce, combine first 3 ingredients, stirring with a whisk until blended. Cover and chill until ready to serve.

2. To prepare falafel, bring ¾ cup water to a boil in a small saucepan; add bulgur to pan. Remove from heat; cover and let stand 30 minutes or until tender. Drain and set aside.

3. Preheat oven to 425°.

4. Place chickpeas and next 9 ingredients in a food processor; pulse 10 times or until well blended and smooth (mixture will be wet). Spoon chickpea mixture into a large bowl; stir in bulgur.

5. Divide mixture into 12 equal portions (a heaping ¼ cup each); shape each portion into a ¼-inch-thick patty. Place patties on a baking sheet coated with cooking spray. Bake at 425° for 10 minutes on each side or until lightly browned. Spread about 2½ tablespoons sauce onto each flatbread. Top each flatbread with 2 falafel patties, 2 tomato slices, and chopped cilantro, if desired. **Yield: 6 servings (serving size: 1 stuffed flatbread).**

CALORIES 388; FAT 7.7g (sat 3.5g, mono 1.6g, poly 1.6g); PROTEIN 18g; CARB 64.6g; FIBER 14.7g; CHOL 7mg; IRON 5.2mg; SODIUM 535mg; CALC 181mg

Focaccia Sandwich with Spring Greens

Focaccia:

8.9 ounces bread flour (about 2 cups)
½ teaspoon sugar
¼ teaspoon salt
1 package dry yeast (about 2¼ teaspoons)
¾ cup very warm water (120° to 130°)
Cooking spray
½ teaspoon olive oil
⅓ cup (1¼-inch) julienne-cut green onions
1 tablespoon (¼ ounce) grated fresh Parmesan cheese
¼ teaspoon black pepper

Sandwich:

4 ounces provolone or Havarti cheese, thinly sliced
8 (¼-inch-thick) slices tomato
3 cups gourmet salad greens
½ cup chopped green onions
2 tablespoons balsamic vinegar
1 tablespoon olive oil
¼ teaspoon salt
⅛ teaspoon black pepper

1. To prepare focaccia, weigh or lightly spoon flour into dry measuring cups; level with a knife. Place flour, sugar, salt, and yeast in a food processor; pulse 2 times or until blended. With processor running, slowly add very warm water through food chute; process until dough leaves sides of bowl and forms a ball. Process an additional 30 seconds. Turn dough out onto a lightly floured surface, and knead lightly 4 to 5 times. Place dough in a large bowl coated with cooking spray, turning to coat top. Cover and let rise in a warm place (85°), free from drafts, 1½ hours or until doubled in size.

2. Punch dough down; let rest 5 minutes. Roll into a 13 x 9–inch rectangle on a lightly floured surface. Transfer dough to a 13 x 9–inch baking pan coated with cooking spray; brush ½ teaspoon oil over dough. Cover and let rise 1½ hours or until puffy.

3. Preheat oven to 400°.

4. Uncover dough. Make indentations in top of dough using the handle of a wooden spoon or your fingertips. Sprinkle ⅓ cup green onions, Parmesan cheese, and ¼ teaspoon pepper over dough, leaving a ½-inch border. Bake at 400° for 20 minutes or until lightly browned. Cool in pan on a wire rack.

5. To prepare sandwich, cut focaccia in half horizontally using a serrated knife; place bottom layer, cut side up, on a flat surface. Arrange provolone cheese and tomato slices over bottom layer; top with salad greens and ½ cup green onions. Combine balsamic vinegar and remaining ingredients in a small bowl, stirring well with a whisk. Drizzle vinaigrette over salad green mixture; top with remaining focaccia layer. Gently press sandwich together; cut into 6 equal portions.

Yield: 6 servings (serving size: 1 [4-inch] square).

CALORIES 278; FAT 9g (sat 3.9g, mono 3.5g, poly 0.8g); PROTEIN 12.1g; CARB 37g; FIBER 1.4g; CHOL 14mg; IRON 3mg; SODIUM 387mg; CALC 186mg

kitchen how-to:
prepare focaccia dough for baking

After the first rise, punch the focaccia dough down, and let it rest for 5 minutes. Roll the dough into a 13 x 9–inch rectangle on a lightly floured surface. Transfer the dough to a 13 x 9–inch baking pan coated with cooking spray. Brush oil over the dough. Cover and let it rise 1½ hours or until puffy. Uncover the dough. Make indentations in the top of the dough using the handle of a wooden spoon or your fingertips. Top with additional herbs, cheese, or seasonings, and bake.

Tartines with Cheese, Peppers, and Chard

A tartine is an open-faced sandwich. This recipe demands a hearty bread (one topped with seeds and intact grains adds a nutrition bonus); it's the best match for the herbed-cheese topping.

- 1 large red bell pepper
- 1 tablespoon olive oil
- 3 cups chopped Swiss chard leaves (about 1 bunch)
- ¼ teaspoon salt
- ⅛ teaspoon crushed red pepper
- ¼ teaspoon black pepper, divided
- 2 garlic cloves, thinly sliced
- 4 (1.5-ounce) slices rustic 100% whole-grain bread
- 2 teaspoons chopped fresh chives
- ½ teaspoon chopped fresh thyme
- 2 ounces soft goat cheese

1. Preheat broiler.
2. Cut bell pepper in half lengthwise; discard seeds and membranes. Place pepper halves, skin sides up, on a foil-lined baking sheet; flatten with hand. Broil 10 minutes or until blackened. Place in a zip-top plastic bag; seal. Let stand 5 minutes. Peel and cut into strips.
3. Heat oil in a large nonstick skillet over medium-high heat. Add chard, salt, crushed red pepper, ⅛ teaspoon black pepper, and garlic to pan; sauté 1½ minutes or until chard wilts, stirring frequently.
4. Arrange bread in a single layer on a baking sheet; broil 3 minutes on each side. Combine chives, thyme, cheese, and remaining ⅛ teaspoon black pepper in a small bowl; spread 2 teaspoons cheese mixture over one side of each bread slice. Arrange roasted pepper slices evenly over cheese; top with chard mixture.
Yield: 2 servings (serving size: 2 tartines).

CALORIES 323; FAT 14.4g (sat 5.1g, mono 6.3g, poly 1g); PROTEIN 12.3g; CARB 43.4g; FIBER 15.2g; CHOL 13mg; IRON 4.2mg; SODIUM 718mg; CALC 330mg

Whole-Grain Bread
What it adds: Whole-grain bread contains the most nutritious part of the grain—the bran, germ, and endosperm, which makes it rich in B vitamins, minerals, and antioxidants.

Grilled Goat Cheese Sandwiches with Fig and Honey

These are equally as good for breakfast or dinner. Mixing honey with the goat cheese makes it easier to spread over the cinnamon-raisin bread.

> 2　teaspoons honey
> ¼　teaspoon grated lemon rind
> 1　(4-ounce) package goat cheese
> 8　(1-ounce) slices cinnamon-raisin bread
> 2　tablespoons fig preserves
> 2　teaspoons thinly sliced fresh basil
> Cooking spray
> 1　teaspoon powdered sugar

1. Combine first 3 ingredients, stirring until well blended. Spread 1 tablespoon goat cheese mixture on each of 4 bread slices; top each slice with 1½ teaspoons preserves and ½ teaspoon basil. Top with remaining bread slices; lightly coat outside of bread with cooking spray.

2. Heat a large nonstick skillet over medium heat. Add 2 sandwiches to pan. Place a cast-iron or heavy skillet on top of sandwiches; press gently to flatten. Cook 3 minutes on each side or until bread is lightly toasted (leave cast-iron skillet on sandwiches while they cook). Repeat with remaining sandwiches. Sprinkle with sugar. **Yield: 4 servings (serving size: 1 sandwich).**

CALORIES 243; FAT 8.5g (sat 4.8g, mono 2.7g, poly 0.5g); PROTEIN 9.8g; CARB 33.1g; FIBER 2.5g; CHOL 13mg; IRON 2.2mg; SODIUM 326mg; CALC 78mg

Aioli
What it adds: This flavorful mayonnaise-based mixture adds tanginess to this vegetable-based sandwich.

Eggplant
What it adds: Eggplant delivers fiber and a little folate. To make the eggplant less bitter and keep it from being overly watery, sprinkle it with salt. Let it stand, applying pressure periodically; rinse it before you grill it.

kitchen how-to:
assemble quick homemade black bean burgers

Bean-based vegetable burgers are filling and packed with nutrition. For more information about creating your own vegetable burger from scratch, see page 291.

1. Place a 2-ounce hamburger bun in a food processor; process 4 times or until the crumbs measure about 1 cup. Transfer the crumbs to a bowl.

2. Combine 1 tablespoon olive oil, 2 teaspoons chopped garlic, and a 15.5-ounce can of black beans that have been rinsed and drained in the food processor; pulse 8 times or until the mixture becomes a thick paste.

3. Scrape the bean mixture into the bowl with the breadcrumbs. Stir in 1 teaspoon grated lime rind, ¾ teaspoon chili powder, ½ teaspoon chopped fresh oregano, ¼ teaspoon salt, 1 large lightly beaten egg, and 1 large lightly beaten egg white.

4. With moistened hands, divide the bean mixture into 4 equal portions (about ⅓ cup per portion). Shape each portion into a 3-inch-wide patty.

Southwest Pinto Bean Burgers with Chipotle Mayonnaise

Burgers:
- ½ cup diced onion
- ½ cup dry breadcrumbs
- ¼ cup chopped cilantro
- 2 tablespoons minced seeded jalapeño pepper
- 2 tablespoons reduced-fat sour cream
- 1 teaspoon hot pepper sauce
- ½ teaspoon ground cumin
- ¼ teaspoon freshly ground black pepper
- ⅛ teaspoon salt
- 1 large egg
- 1 (15-ounce) can pinto beans, drained
- 1 (8¾-ounce) can no salt-added whole-kernel corn, drained

Chipotle Mayonnaise:
- ¼ cup low-fat mayonnaise
- 1 teaspoon canned minced chipotle chile in adobo sauce

Remaining Ingredients:
- 1 tablespoon canola oil
- 4 (1½-ounce) whole-wheat hamburger buns, toasted
- 4 romaine lettuce leaves

1. To prepare burgers, combine first 10 ingredients in a bowl. Add pinto beans and corn; partially mash with a fork. Divide bean mixture into 4 equal portions, shaping each portion into a 3½-inch patty, and refrigerate 10 minutes.

2. To prepare chipotle mayonnaise, combine mayonnaise and 1 teaspoon chipotle in a small bowl; set aside.

3. Heat canola oil in a large nonstick skillet over medium-high heat. Add patties to pan, and cook 4 minutes on each side or until thoroughly heated. Place patties on bottom halves of buns; top each patty with 1 tablespoon mayonnaise, 1 lettuce leaf, and top half of bun. **Yield: 4 servings.**

CALORIES 411; FAT 10.7g (sat 1.9g, mono 3.2g, poly 3.2g); PROTEIN 15.2g; CARB 63.1g; FIBER 9.1g; CHOL 57mg; IRON 3.9mg; SODIUM 837mg; CALC 153mg

Middle Eastern Chickpea Miniburgers

Serve each burger on a whole-grain slider bun with lettuce, crisp radish slices, roasted red bell pepper, and canola-based mayonnaise.

  1 (8-ounce) red potato
  3 tablespoons olive oil, divided
  1 teaspoon minced garlic
  1 (15.5-ounce) can chickpeas (garbanzo beans), rinsed, drained, and divided
  1 tablespoon chopped fresh parsley
  ½ teaspoon salt
  ½ teaspoon grated lemon rind
  ½ teaspoon smoked paprika
  ¼ teaspoon freshly ground black pepper
  2 large egg whites, lightly beaten

1. Place potato in a saucepan; cover with water. Bring to a boil; cook 20 minutes or until very tender. Drain. Cool slightly. Coarsely chop, and place in medium bowl. Add 1 tablespoon oil and garlic to bowl; mash potato mixture with a potato masher until slightly chunky. Remove 3 tablespoons chickpeas; place in a small bowl. Add remaining chickpeas to potato mixture; mash until well blended. Stir in reserved 3 tablespoons whole chickpeas, parsley, and next 5 ingredients. With moistened hands, divide mixture into 6 equal portions (about ⅓ cup mixture per portion), shaping each into a 3-inch patty.

2. Heat 1 tablespoon oil in a large nonstick skillet over medium-high heat. Add 3 patties to pan; reduce heat to medium, and cook 4 minutes or until bottoms are golden. Carefully turn patties over; cook 3 minutes or until bottoms are golden and patties are set. Repeat procedure with remaining 1 tablespoon oil and 3 patties.

Yield: 3 servings (serving size: 2 patties).

CALORIES 308; FAT 16.2g (sat 1.9g, mono 10.9g, poly 3g); PROTEIN 9g; CARB 32.9g; FIBER 6.5g; CHOL 0mg; IRON 2.6mg; SODIUM 716mg; CALC 54mg

Grilled Lemon-Basil Tofu Burgers

The olive-garlic mayonnaise on this sandwich adds a Mediterranean flavor. Serve it with grilled asparagus.

⅓ cup finely chopped fresh basil
2 tablespoons Dijon mustard
2 tablespoons honey
2 teaspoons grated lemon rind
¼ cup fresh lemon juice
1 tablespoon extra-virgin olive oil
½ teaspoon salt
¼ teaspoon freshly ground black pepper
4 garlic cloves, minced and divided
1 pound firm or extra-firm tofu, drained
Cooking spray
⅓ cup finely chopped pitted kalamata olives
3 tablespoons reduced-fat sour cream
3 tablespoons light mayonnaise
6 (1½-ounce) hamburger buns
6 (¼-inch-thick) slices tomato
1 cup trimmed watercress

1. Combine first 8 ingredients and 3 garlic cloves in a small bowl. Cut tofu crosswise into 6 slices. Pat each square dry with paper towels. Place tofu slices on a jelly-roll pan. Brush both sides of tofu slices with lemon juice mixture; reserve remaining juice mixture. Let tofu stand 1 hour.
2. Prepare grill.
3. Place tofu slices on grill rack coated with cooking spray; grill 3 minutes on each side. Brush tofu with reserved juice mixture.
4. Combine remaining 1 minced garlic clove, chopped olives, sour cream, and mayonnaise in a small bowl; stir well. Spread about 1½ tablespoons mayonnaise mixture over bottom half of each hamburger bun; top each serving with 1 tofu slice, 1 tomato slice, about 2 tablespoons watercress, and top half of bun. **Yield: 6 servings (serving size: 1 burger).**

CALORIES 276; FAT 11.3g (sat 1.9g, mono 5.7g, poly 2.2g); PROTEIN 10.5g; CARB 34.5g; FIBER 1.5g; CHOL 5mg; IRON 2.4mg; SODIUM 743mg; CALC 101mg

kitchen how-to: grill tofu

Marinating the tofu adds flavor and also helps the tofu slices acquire a golden crust when grilled. You may want to reserve the marinade to baste the tofu with while it grills.

1. Remove the tofu from the marinade, and place them on a grill pan or a grill rack coated with cooking spray.
2. Grill the tofu for 3 minutes on each side.
3. While the tofu grills, brush it with the reserved marinade.

Portobello Cheeseburgers

Portobello mushrooms pair well with pungent Gorgonzola cheese. Use crumbled blue cheese to save even more time.

2 teaspoons olive oil
4 (4-inch) portobello caps
¼ teaspoon salt
¼ teaspoon black pepper
1 tablespoon bottled minced garlic
¼ cup (1 ounce) crumbled Gorgonzola cheese
3 tablespoons reduced-fat mayonnaise
4 (2-ounce) sandwich rolls
2 cups trimmed arugula
½ cup sliced bottled roasted red bell peppers

1. Heat oil in a large nonstick skillet over medium-high heat. Sprinkle mushrooms with salt and pepper. Add mushrooms to pan; sauté 4 minutes or until tender, turning once. Add garlic to pan; sauté 30 seconds. Remove from heat.

2. Combine cheese and mayonnaise, stirring well. Spread about 2 tablespoons mayonnaise mixture over bottom half of each roll; top each serving with ½ cup arugula and 2 tablespoons peppers. Place 1 mushroom on each serving, and top with top halves of rolls.

Yield: 4 servings (serving size: 1 burger).

CALORIES 278; FAT 9.9g (sat 3g, mono 1.7g, poly 0.4g); PROTEIN 9.3g; CARB 33.7g; FIBER 2.4g; CHOL 6mg; IRON 1.7mg; SODIUM 726mg; CALC 129mg

kitchen how-to: sauté portobellos

Portobellos have a firm texture and hearty flavor. Sautéing them helps bring out their earthy, smoky flavor.

1. Heat the oil in a large nonstick skillet over medium-high heat.

2. Sprinkle the mushrooms with salt and pepper or any other seasonings you'd like.

3. Add the mushrooms to the pan.

4. Sauté the mushrooms for 4 minutes or until tender, turning once.

{ vegan recipe }

Tempeh Fajitas

Use a wire grill basket to cook the onion and bell pepper slices so they don't fall into the grill. If there's enough room on the grill, you can heat the tortillas while the onion mixture and tempeh cook. Wrap the tortillas in heavy-duty foil, and grill them for 5 minutes or until they're thoroughly heated.

    1   (8-ounce) package five-grain tempeh
    1   cup pineapple juice
    ¼   cup less-sodium soy sauce
    2   tablespoons fresh lime juice
    2   teaspoons ground cumin
    2   teaspoons canola oil
    ½   teaspoon freshly ground black pepper, divided
    1   garlic clove, minced
    2   cups (½-inch) vertically sliced onion
 1½   cups (½-inch-thick) sliced green bell pepper
        Cooking spray
    ¼   teaspoon salt
    4   (8-inch) whole-wheat tortillas
    ¼   cup chipotle salsa (such as Frontera)

1. Cut tempeh in half crosswise; cut each half length-wise into 6 strips. Place tempeh in a shallow dish. Combine pineapple juice, soy sauce, lime juice, cumin, oil, ¼ teaspoon black pepper, and garlic in a small saucepan; bring to a boil. Pour pineapple juice mixture over tempeh. Marinate at room temperature 30 minutes or up to 2 hours in the refrigerator.

2. Prepare grill.

3. Lightly coat onion and bell pepper with cooking spray; sprinkle with salt and remaining ¼ teaspoon black pepper. Arrange onion mixture in a wire grilling basket coated with cooking spray. Place grilling basket on grill rack; grill 5 minutes or until lightly browned, turning occasionally. Remove the tempeh from marinade, reserving marinade. Place tempeh on grill rack coated with cooking spray; grill 2 minutes on each side or until lightly browned, basting occasionally with reserved marinade.

4. Warm tortillas according to package directions. Arrange 3 tempeh pieces, ½ cup onion mixture, and 1 tablespoon salsa down center of each tortilla; roll up.

Yield: 4 servings (serving size: 1 fajita).

CALORIES 259; FAT 5.1g (sat 0.7g, mono 1.2g, poly 2.2g); PROTEIN 14.6g; CARB 47.3g; FIBER 8g; CHOL 0mg; IRON 3.1mg; SODIUM 712mg; CALC 64mg

kitchen how-to: grill tempeh

Grilling tempeh creates an irresistible smoky flavor and a delicious golden brown crust. You can also prepare tempeh inside in a grill pan, but it won't have the same smoky flavor an outdoor charcoal grill creates. To create an extra layer of flavor, marinate the tempeh before grilling it. Try using one of the more mellow tempeh varieties—the grains, which can include brown rice and quinoa, blended with the soybeans let the flavors in the marinade come through more.

1. Cut the tempeh in half crosswise.
2. Cut each half lengthwise into 6 strips.
3. If you'd like to marinate the tempeh, place the tempeh in a shallow dish with the marinade. Let it marinate at room temperature for 30 minutes or up to 2 hours in the refrigerator.
4. Remove the tempeh from the marinade. You can discard the marinade or use it to baste the tempeh slices as they grill for additional flavor. Place the tempeh on a grill pan or grill rack coated with cooking spray; grill 2 minutes on each side or until lightly browned.
5. As the tempeh slices cook, baste them occasionally with the reserved marinade.

Three-Grain Tempeh
What it adds: This variety, which is made with brown rice, barley, and millet, is light and mellow. You can use any variety that you like.

Barbecue Sauce
What it adds: This homemade barbecue sauce adds a sweet and spicy flavor to the tempeh.

Barbecued Tempeh Sandwiches Smothered with Peppers and Onions

⅓ cup ketchup
1 tablespoon brown sugar
1½ teaspoons vegetable oil
1½ teaspoons cider vinegar
1 teaspoon Dijon mustard
¼ teaspoon chili powder
¼ teaspoon less-sodium soy sauce
¼ teaspoon hot sauce
1 garlic clove, minced
1 (8-ounce) package three-grain tempeh
1 red bell pepper, cut in half
1 yellow bell pepper, cut in half
1 red onion, cut into ½-inch-thick slices
Cooking spray
4 (1½-ounce) hamburger buns

1. Prepare grill.

2. Combine first 9 ingredients in a small bowl, stirring with a whisk.

3. Cut tempeh in half lengthwise; cut slices in half crosswise. Cut each tempeh slice in half horizontally to form 8 slices. Brush tempeh slices, bell peppers, and onion with ketchup mixture. Place on grill rack coated with cooking spray; grill 4 minutes on each side or until tempeh is thoroughly heated. Remove tempeh, bell peppers, and onion from grill. Cut bell peppers into ½-inch-wide strips; separate onions into rings.

4. Place 2 tempeh slices on bottom half of each bun. Top tempeh slices with one-fourth of bell peppers, one-fourth of onion, and top half of bun. **Yield: 4 servings (serving size: 1 sandwich).**

CALORIES 309; FAT 8.7g (sat 1.5g, mono 1.9g, poly 4.5g); PROTEIN 15.6g; CARB 45.2g; FIBER 3g; CHOL 0mg; IRON 3.6mg; SODIUM 531mg; CALC 130mg

{ vegan recipe }
Tofu Banh Mi

Serve with Sriracha (hot chile sauce) if you prefer more fire.

- 1 (14-ounce) package water-packed firm tofu, drained
- 2 tablespoons less-sodium soy sauce
- 2 teaspoons finely grated peeled fresh ginger
- ⅓ cup rice vinegar
- ¼ cup sugar
- 1 teaspoon kosher salt
- 1¼ cups (3-inch) matchstick-cut carrot
- 1 cup sliced shiitake mushroom caps
- ¼ teaspoon freshly ground black pepper
- 1 julienne-cut green onion
- 1 cucumber, peeled, halved lengthwise, and thinly sliced (about 2 cups)
- 2 tablespoons canola oil
- 1 (12-ounce) loaf French bread
- ½ cup fresh cilantro sprigs
- 2 jalapeño peppers, thinly sliced

1. Cut tofu crosswise into 8 (½-inch-thick) slices. Arrange tofu on several layers of paper towels. Top with several more layers of paper towels; top with a cast-iron skillet or other heavy pan. Let stand 30 minutes. Remove tofu from paper towels.

2. Combine soy sauce and ginger in a 13 x 9–inch baking dish. Arrange tofu slices in a single layer in soy mixture. Cover and refrigerate 8 hours or overnight, turning once.

3. Combine vinegar, sugar, and salt in a medium bowl, stirring until sugar and salt dissolve. Add carrot and next 4 ingredients; toss well. Let stand 30 minutes, stirring occasionally. Drain carrot mixture through a sieve; drain thoroughly.

4. Heat oil in a large nonstick skillet over medium-high heat. Remove tofu from marinade; discard marinade. Pat tofu slices dry with paper towels. Add tofu slices to pan; sauté 4 minutes on each side or until crisp and golden.

5. Preheat broiler.

6. Cut bread in half lengthwise. Open halves, laying bread cut side up on a baking sheet. Broil 2 minutes or until lightly browned. Place tofu slices on bottom half of bread; top with carrot mixture, cilantro, and jalapeño slices. Top with top half of bread. Cut loaf crosswise into 6 equal pieces.

Yield: 6 servings (serving size: 1 sandwich).

CALORIES 369; FAT 14.1g (sat 1.8g, mono 5.2g, poly 6.1g); PROTEIN 11.9g; CARB 49.6g; FIBER 5g; CHOL 0mg; IRON 2.6mg; SODIUM 367mg; CALC 147mg

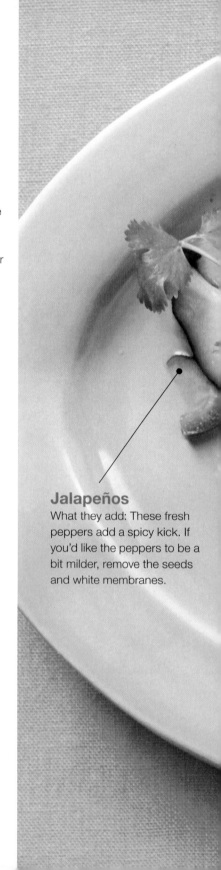

Jalapeños

What they add: These fresh peppers add a spicy kick. If you'd like the peppers to be a bit milder, remove the seeds and white membranes.

Fresh Cilantro

What it adds: This fresh herb adds a slight citrusy flavor to this sandwich.

Marinated Tofu

What it adds: Allow 8 hours to marinate the tofu—it soaks up savory flavor from the soy sauce and heat from the fresh ginger for this riff on a popular Vietnamese sandwich.

way to cook vegetarian
sides

sides

Vegetarian side dishes are a delicious way to round out your meal. Not only do they bring new flavors to your plate, but they can also bring a boost of nutrition.

Keep It Colorful

Nutritionally, sides can be an excellent way to add more vitamins, minerals, and antioxidants to your diet. The key is to aim for variety based on color—the compounds that give plants their color work as immune boosters, antioxidants, and anti-inflammatories in humans. Plus, the deeper the color, the more of these beneficial compounds the plant contains. The best advice: Choose fruits and vegetables of all colors to obtain the widest variety of nutrients.

Side Sense

It's easy to get into the routine of preparing the same vegetables and side dishes, but it's easy to break out of the routine once you implement a few strategies. First, there is nothing wrong with repeating favorite vegetables. The trick is to pair new flavors with familiar ingredients. It also helps to try new vegetables from time to time. Here are a few other tips:

• **Double or triple vegetables.** Combining two or three vegetables adds appeal. Mix peppers, onions, and spinach in a simple sauté, or roast a few vegetables with chopped herbs, shallots, and garlic. Vary the shape, color, taste, and texture of ingredients to boost interest.

• **Try new ingredients.** If black-eyed peas, red lentils, kohlrabi, or rutabagas are unfamiliar to you, try them. Experiment with one new ingredient a week. Each new food you enjoy broadens your options.

• **Use familiar vegetables in different ways.** Even your favorite side dishes may begin to become boring if you prepare them the same way time after time. Keep them interesting by using new flavors or cooking techniques. Instead of boiling corn on the cob, try preparing it on the grill for a new flavor, or mix up the seasoning blend you traditionally use to prepare your steamed broccoli, and use it on corn as well as other vegetables.

• **Sauce it.** Veggies can change personality with the addition of vinaigrettes or ethnic condiments. Try tossing mixed vegetables with pesto or white balsamic vinaigrette or spicing up potatoes with a tablespoon or two of chutney.

kitchen how-to: grill corn

When buying fresh corn, always purchase it with the husks on since they help retain the corn's natural moisture. To shuck the corn, hold each ear with the tip facing down, and pull the husks and silks up toward your body. You'll want to wipe the shucked corn with a damp paper towel to remove any remaining silks. Grilling is a great way to cook corn on the cob since it intensifies the natural sweetness.

1. Place the shucked corn on a grill rack coated with cooking spray.
2. Grill the corn 10 minutes, turning it frequently to prevent one side from overcooking.

kitchen how-to: blanch vegetables

1

2

Blanching maintains a vegetable's vibrant color and helps set its flavor. Blanching involves placing vegetables into boiling water to cook them quickly, and then plunging them in ice water to stop the cooking process.

1. Drop the vegetables into rapidly boiling water, and cook until crisp-tender. Time will vary depending on the vegetable, but cook time could be as short as 1 minute.
2. Drain the vegetables, and plunge them into ice water to stop the cooking process. Drain them well.

kitchen how-to: easily peel cipollini onions

Pearl onions or boiling onions also work well in this application.

1. Trim the tops and root ends of the onions.
2. Cook the onions in boiling water for 2 minutes. Remove the onions using a slotted spoon.
3. Plunge the onions into ice water to stop the cooking process. Drain them well.
4. Let the onions cool before you peel them.

Beer-Battered Onion Rings

Unless you happen to have an open can of beer in your refrigerator, try this simple way to flatten the suds you need for this batter: Pour ½ cup of beer into a small bowl, and stir it with a fork—you'll be left with about ⅓ cup of flat beer.

> 2 **large onions (about 1½ pounds), peeled**
> ⅔ **cup all-purpose flour**
> ½ **teaspoon salt**
> ¼ **teaspoon paprika**
> ¼ **teaspoon freshly ground black pepper**
> ⅓ **cup flat beer**
> 1 **large egg white, lightly beaten**
> 1½ **tablespoons vegetable oil, divided**
>   **Cooking spray**
> ¼ **cup ketchup**

1. Preheat oven to 400°.

2. Cut onions crosswise into ¾-inch-thick slices, and separate into rings. Use 16 of the largest rings; reserve remaining onion rings for another use. Lightly spoon flour into a dry measuring cup; level with a knife. Combine flour, salt, paprika, and pepper in a medium bowl. Stir in beer and egg white (batter will be thick). Heat 1½ teaspoons oil in a large nonstick skillet over medium-high heat. Dip 5 onion rings into batter, letting excess drip off. Add onion rings to pan; cook 2 minutes on each side or until golden. Place onion rings on a jelly-roll pan. Repeat procedure with remaining onion rings, batter, and oil. Coat onion rings with cooking spray. Bake at 400° for 10 minutes or until crisp. Serve rings with ketchup. **Yield: 4 servings (serving size: 4 onion rings and 1 tablespoon ketchup).**

CALORIES 209; FAT 5.8g (sat 1g, mono 1.6g, poly 2.7g); PROTEIN 5.1g; CARB 34.1g; FIBER 3.7g; CHOL 0mg; IRON 1.5mg; SODIUM 490mg; CALC 39mg

kitchen how-to: make beer-battered onion rings

Cut the onions crosswise into ¾-inch-thick slices, and separate the slices into rings. Use 16 of the largest rings, and reserve the remaining onion rings for another use.

1. Prepare the batter. Heat 1½ teaspoons oil in a large nonstick skillet over medium-high heat. Dip 5 of the onion rings into the batter, letting the excess drip off.

2. Add the onion rings to the pan; cook for 2 minutes on each side or until golden. Place the onion rings on a jelly-roll pan. Repeat the procedure of dipping the remaining onion rings into the batter and cooking them in the remaining oil. Coat the onion rings with cooking spray, and bake them at 400° for 10 minutes or until they're crisp.

all about buying & storing onions

Onions should have dry, papery skins with no signs of spotting, sprouting, or softness. Store them in a cool, dry, well-ventilated area for up to two months. Once you've cut onions, you can refrigerate them in an airtight container for up to four days.

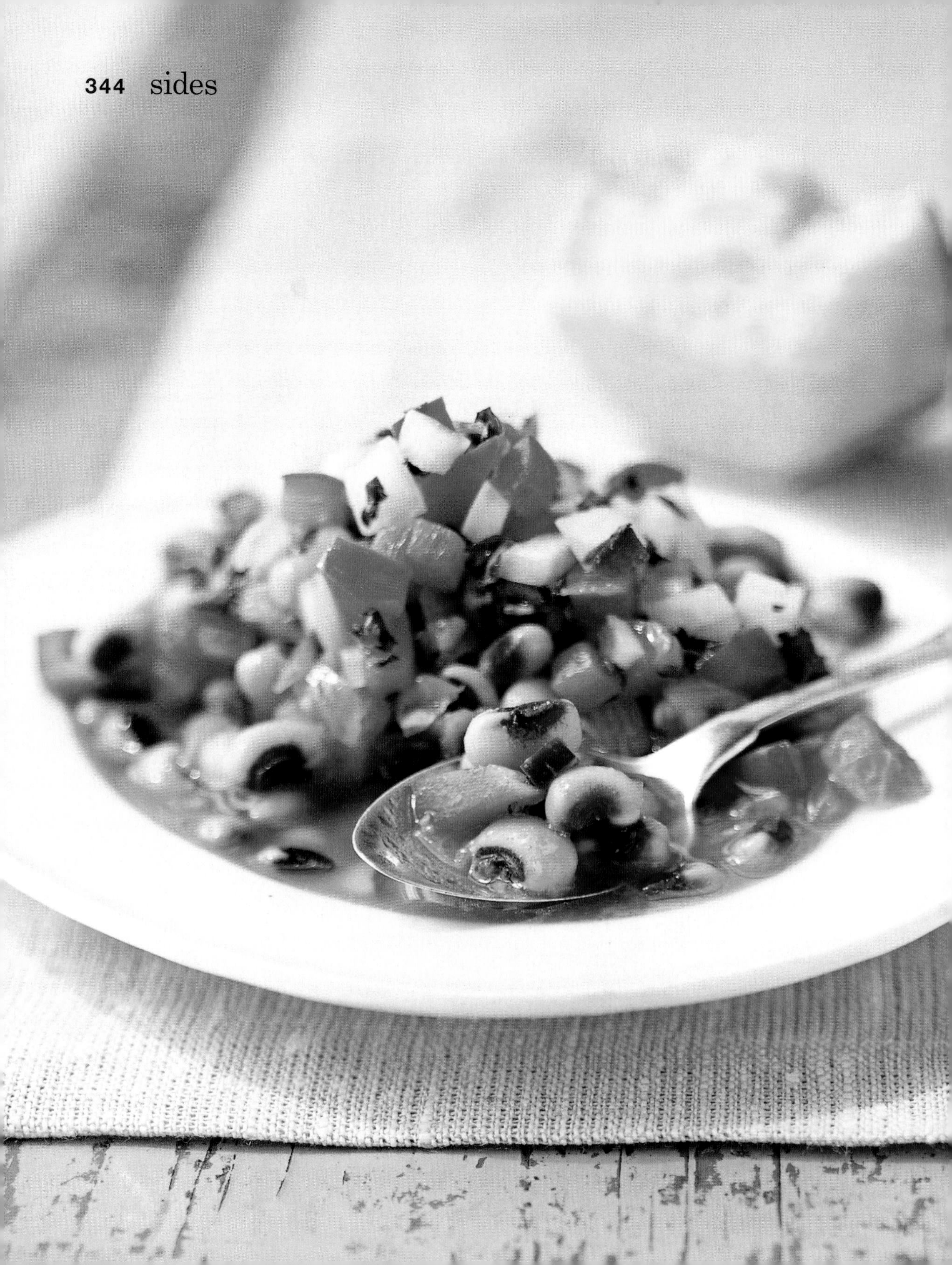

{vegan recipe}
Fresh Peas with Spicy Pepper Relish

The lightly pickled relish will keep for up to two days in the refrigerator. Corn muffins with honey butter make a great accompaniment.

Relish:
- 1 cup diced red bell pepper
- ½ cup diced onion
- 2 tablespoons chopped fresh parsley
- 1 tablespoon cider vinegar
- 2 teaspoons minced seeded jalapeño pepper
- ½ teaspoon sugar
- ¼ teaspoon dry mustard
- ¼ teaspoon salt

Peas:
- 3 cups fresh black-eyed peas
- 2 teaspoons olive oil
- 1 cup chopped onion
- ¼ teaspoon minced garlic
- 2½ cups organic vegetable broth
- ½ teaspoon ground cumin
- ½ teaspoon Spanish smoked paprika
- ¼ teaspoon ground red pepper
- ¼ teaspoon salt
- 1 bay leaf

1. To prepare relish, combine first 8 ingredients in a bowl. Cover and chill.
2. To prepare peas, sort and wash peas; set aside. Heat oil in a medium saucepan over medium-high heat. Add 1 cup onion and garlic to pan; sauté 5 minutes. Stir in peas, broth, and remaining ingredients; bring to a boil. Cover, reduce heat, and simmer 20 minutes or until peas are tender. Discard bay leaf. Serve with relish.
Yield: 6 servings (serving size: ⅔ cup peas and 2 tablespoons relish).

CALORIES 113; FAT 2g (sat 0.3g, mono 1.2g, poly 0.3g); PROTEIN 2.9g; CARB 21.3g; FIBER 4.8g; CHOL 0mg; IRON 1.2mg; SODIUM 440mg; CALC 106mg

kitchen how-to:
freeze field peas

Field peas add earthy flavor, protein, and fiber to your plate. Most varieties, such as black-eyed, crowder, and lady peas, are available fresh from May to early August, which makes those months the ideal time to freeze them for year-round enjoyment.

1. Snap off the end of each pod. For some peas sold in supermarkets, the vein (the string that runs along the length of the pod) has already been removed. If the vein is still on the peas, just pull it gently—don't tug it.
2. Press gently against the pod's seam with your finger to open it, and then gingerly run your finger down the inside back of the pod to pop out the peas. Discard the pod plus any wilted, discolored, or damaged peas.
3. To freeze, fill a heavy-duty freezer bag with the peas, and place it in the freezer. Do not wash the peas before freezing them; water frozen inside the bag could make the peas mushy when they're thawed. For the best taste, use the peas within three months. To thaw the peas, place the frozen bags in the refrigerator for a few hours. You can also place the peas in a colander and run cold water over them until they're thawed.

kitchen how-to: make stuffed potato skins

You can bake the potatoes up to two days ahead and fill them with stuffing. Cover and store them in the refrigerator. Before serving, let them stand at room temperature for 30 minutes, sprinkle them with cheese, and bake them.

1. Pierce each potato with a fork. Bake the potatoes at 400° for 1 hour or until tender. Cut them in half lengthwise.

2. Scoop out the flesh from each potato, leaving about a ¼-inch-thick shell.

3. Combine the potato flesh with milk or buttermilk (or both) and sour cream, and mash the mixture with a potato masher to the desired consistency. Stir in any mix of seasonings you'd like: cheese, fresh herbs, butter, salt, and pepper.

4. Divide the mixture evenly among the potato shells. Place the stuffed potatoes in a single layer on a baking sheet; sprinkle them evenly with cheese, and bake them at 400° for 12 minutes or until they're heated. Preheat the broiler. Broil the stuffed potatoes 2 minutes or until they're browned and bubbly.

{ vegan recipe }

Indian-Spiced Grilled Baby Squash

Grilling underscores the earthiness of the cumin and coriander, and it also enhances the nuttiness of this summer squash. For the most colorful skewers, use white, orange, or yellow pattypan squash.

- 1 tablespoon olive oil
- 1 teaspoon grated peeled fresh ginger
- ½ teaspoon salt
- ½ teaspoon ground coriander
- ¼ teaspoon ground cumin
- 1 pound baby pattypan squash, cut in half crosswise
- 1 medium red onion, cut into 1-inch pieces
- Cooking spray
- 1 tablespoon fresh lemon juice
- 1 tablespoon thinly sliced fresh mint leaves

1. Preheat grill.
2. Combine first 7 ingredients in a large bowl; toss well. Thread squash and onion alternately onto each of 8 (10-inch) skewers. Place skewers on grill rack coated with cooking spray; grill 10 minutes or until tender, turning frequently. Drizzle with juice. Sprinkle with mint.
Yield: 4 servings (serving size: 2 skewers).

CALORIES 61; FAT 3.6g (sat 0.5g, mono 2.5g, poly 0.5g); PROTEIN 1.7g; CARB 6.9g; FIBER 1.8g; CHOL 0mg; IRON 0.6mg; SODIUM 299mg; CALC 26mg

all about baby squash

As with their full-grown counterparts, baby summer squash are best enjoyed during their peak season of early to late summer. Baby squash varieties include miniature versions of the popular yellow and zucchini squashes, as well as the more exotic-looking pattypan and scallopini, which resemble flattened, scallop-shaped saucers. Baby squash boast a mildly sweet, nutty flavor and tender flesh. Choose baby squash that have shiny, bright-colored skin, and avoid those that have spots, bruises, or cracks. Store baby squash in a perforated plastic bag in the refrigerator for no more than five days.

Zucchini Boats with Ricotta-Basil Mousse

Use the fragrant cheese stuffing with any mild vegetable, such as bell peppers, mushroom caps, baby eggplant, or tomatoes. Save the scooped-out zucchini pulp for risotto or pasta sauce. You can use a mini chopper to chop the herbs quickly, but do not use it to combine the mousse ingredients because it will liquefy the ricotta. Use our recipe for Homemade Ricotta Cheese on page 148, if you'd like.

    6 small zucchini (about 1½ pounds)
    Cooking spray
    1 cup loosely packed fresh basil leaves,
       finely chopped
    1 cup (8 ounces) ricotta cheese
    ½ cup loosely packed fresh flat-leaf parsley
       leaves, finely chopped
    ¼ cup (1 ounce) grated fresh Parmigiano-
       Reggiano cheese
    2 tablespoons hot water
    1 tablespoon fresh lemon juice
    ¼ teaspoon salt
    ¼ teaspoon freshly ground black pepper
    Parsley sprigs (optional)

1. Preheat oven to 450°.
2. Cut each zucchini in half lengthwise; scoop out pulp, leaving a ¼-inch-thick shell. Reserve pulp for another use. Arrange zucchini shells in a single layer in a 13 x 9–inch baking dish coated with cooking spray.
3. Combine basil and next 7 ingredients, stirring well with a whisk. Divide mixture evenly among shells, pressing gently. Bake at 450° for 20 minutes or until zucchini is tender. Garnish with parsley, if desired.
Yield: 12 servings (serving size: 1 stuffed shell).

CALORIES 59; FAT 2.8g (sat 1.7g, mono 0.8g, poly 0.2g); PROTEIN 5.5g; CARB 3.5g;
FIBER 0.8g; CHOL 9mg; IRON 0.5mg; SODIUM 158mg; CALC 129mg

kitchen how-to:
hollow zucchini

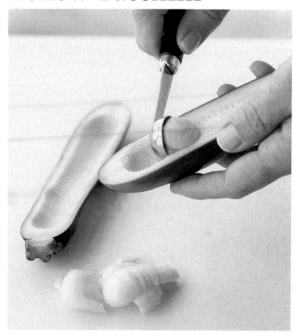

To easily scoop out the zucchini halves for the herbed mousse, use a melon baller. If you don't have one, use a small spoon instead.

way to cook vegetarian

soups
& stews

soups & stews

Soups and stews are basic, and the techniques are classic. Each is based on a flavorful liquid, such as stock or broth, and any additional ingredients contribute specific flavors or textures. They make wonderful vegetarian meals because they typically rely on affordable—even homegrown ingredients—such as hearty grains and vegetables.

Stocks and Broths

These flavorful liquids form the base of most soups. Some rich soups may use milk or cream or a combination of dairy and stock or broth as their base, but homemade stocks and broths are ideal. It's well worth the time investment and extra work to make them because they provide fresh, pure flavor and a lower sodium content than many store-bought varieties. See pages 79, 391, and 401 for recipes you can use to create homemade stocks and broths.

If you don't have time to make your own from scratch, you can choose a suitable stock or broth from a variety of store-bought brands. Many of them are high in sodium though, so be sure to look for one that contains 700 milligrams or less of sodium per cup.

Ice-cube trays offer an excellent and easy option for storing stocks and broths. Simply pour the liquid into the trays, and freeze them; you can transfer the frozen cubes to a plastic zip-top freezer bag for easy access (one cube equals about 2 tablespoons). Another space-efficient way to store stock or broth is to pour it into plastic zip-top freezer bags and freeze.

simple vegetable stock, page 401

roasted vegetable stock, page 391

mushroom stock, page 79

Adding Dimension

The next step when making soups and stews is to choose the vegetables, herbs, and spices, which are another way to add extra dimension and flavor. To deepen their flavor and create a more flavorful soup or stew, sauté aromatic vegetables, such as carrots, onion, and celery, in oil or butter until they're golden brown before adding the liquid to the pot.

The next step is deglazing (adding liquid after sautéing the vegetables and scraping the pan to remove the tasty and flavorful browned bits). Acidic ingredients, such as wine or vinegar, are often used for deglazing, and most of the liquid evaporates as it cooks, leaving behind a concentrated flavor.

When you add the stock or broth, it becomes infused with the flavors of the vegetables as it simmers. At this step for soups, you can choose to completely puree them for a smoother texture (see Kitchen How-to: Make Healthy Creamy Soups on page 382 for more information), partially puree them to thicken the soup a little, or leave them as is for a chunkier soup.

Freezing and Thawing

You want to make sure you properly freeze food so it still tastes good once it's thawed and reheated. To help ensure quality, completely cool a soup or stew before packaging it. You can eliminate freezer burn by using freezer-appropriate containers, such as rigid plastic containers with lids or heavy-duty zip-top plastic bags specifically labeled for freezing. You can prevent ice crystals (shown above), which can alter the flavor and texture, by freezing the soup or stew in appropriate-sized containers: Don't allow for much air space in the container, and fill the container almost to the top; if you are using zip-top plastic bags, squeeze out as much air as possible.

To thaw, place the frozen soup or stew in the refrigerator to defrost overnight. To prevent the ingredients from becoming mushy, reheat thawed soups and stews over medium-low to medium heat.

Customizing Stocks and Broths

If you have a specific dish in mind, you can customize the stock or broth to the dish. Most of our stocks and broths call for fresh thyme and parsley sprigs, black peppercorns, and bay leaves to balance their flavor. To tailor them to suit your tastes:
• Substitute your favorite fresh herbs in place of thyme or parsley.

• For a more pronounced garlic flavor, peel and crush the cloves before simmering them with the stock or broth.
• For an Asian-style stock or broth, simmer it with ginger, and add 2 tablespoons of less-sodium soy sauce after straining it.
• For a fiery stock or broth, add 1 or 2 halved chiles as it simmers.

soups

Great soups start with a flavorful liquid, usually stock or broth. Additional ingredients can be added to create delicious soups with their own unique combinations of flavors and textures.

Garlic Soup *(Sopa de Ajo)*

This simple appetizer soup (SOH-pah day AH-ho) makes the most of everyday ingredients. Use high-quality ingredients because this basic soup has few elements, and each contributes substantially to its success. Serve it with a slice of toast and a green salad for a light lunch.

    2 teaspoons olive oil
    5 tablespoons minced garlic
    1 teaspoon sweet smoked paprika
    3 cups organic vegetable broth (such as Emeril's)
    1 cup water
    ¼ teaspoon salt
    ¼ teaspoon freshly ground black pepper
    2 (1-ounce) slices rustic bread, cut into 1-inch
       cubes
    8 large eggs
    2 tablespoons chopped fresh flat-leaf parsley

1. Preheat broiler.

2. Heat oil in a large saucepan over medium heat. Add garlic to pan; cook 5 minutes or until tender (do not brown). Stir in paprika. Add broth and next 3 ingredients; bring to a boil. Reduce heat, and simmer 10 minutes.

3. Arrange bread cubes in a single layer on a baking sheet; broil 4 minutes or until golden, stirring once halfway through cooking. Reduce oven temperature to 350°.

4. Place about ¼ cup bread cubes in each of 8 oven-proof soup bowls. Break one egg into each bowl; ladle about ½ cup broth mixture into each bowl. Arrange bowls on a baking sheet; bake at 350° for 20 minutes or until egg whites are set but yolks are still runny. Sprinkle evenly with chopped parsley. **Yield: 8 servings.**

CALORIES 114; FAT 5.2g (sat 1.3g, mono 2.7g, poly 0.9g); PROTEIN 7.3g; CARB 7.6g; FIBER 0.3g; CHOL 180mg; IRON 1.3mg; SODIUM 398mg; CALC 38mg

kitchen how-to:
mince garlic

Minced garlic suffuses dishes with vivid flavor, whether raw in a vinaigrette or briefly sautéed for a sauce.

1. To loosen the papery skin from garlic, place the flat side of a knife on the clove. Press down using the heel of your hand, or lightly tap the knife with your fist to break and loosen the skin.

2. Peel off the papery skin, and slice off the tough end with a knife.

3. To mince the garlic, make thin, lengthwise cuts through the clove, and then cut the strips crosswise.

kitchen how-to:
clean & freeze rhubarb

Because of its short growing season (the bulk of the crop arrives in April and May), rhubarb is a much-sought-after spring commodity. When buying, look for deep-red, crisp stalks, free of blemishes and cuts, and then follow these instructions for prepping and freezing the rhubarb. You'll have plenty of its tart sweetness on hand to use during the off-season months.

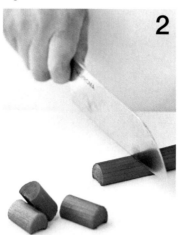

1. Trim the leaves from the top of the stalk; cut about an inch from the bottom, and discard it.
2. Rinse the stalks, and pat them dry with a towel. Cut the stalks into 1-inch sections. You can use the stalks fresh as is, or read on for freezing directions.
3. Lay the cut pieces on a lined baking sheet, and freeze them for about an hour to prevent the pieces from sticking together.
4. Transfer the pieces to a zip-top plastic bag, and store them in the freezer for up to six months. When you are ready to use the rhubarb, defrost it overnight in the refrigerator.

Rhubarb-Lentil Soup with Crème Fraîche

1½ **cups boiling water**
¾ **cup dried petite green lentils**
    Cooking spray
2 **cups finely chopped carrot**
1¾ **cups finely chopped celery**
1½ **cups finely chopped red onion**
¼ **cup chopped fresh parsley**
2 **cups chopped rhubarb (about 12 ounces)**
4 **cups organic vegetable broth**
½ **teaspoon salt**
¼ **teaspoon freshly ground black pepper**
1 **tablespoon chopped fresh dill**
6 **tablespoons crème fraîche**
    Dill sprigs (optional)

1. Pour 1½ cups boiling water over lentils in a small bowl; let stand 10 minutes.

2. Heat a Dutch oven over medium-high heat; coat pan with cooking spray. Add carrot and next 3 ingredients to pan; sauté 4 minutes. Add rhubarb, and sauté 3 minutes. Drain lentils, and add lentils to pan. Stir in broth and salt; bring to a boil. Cover, reduce heat, and simmer 35 minutes or until lentils are tender.

3. Remove from heat; let cool 5 minutes. Place 3 cups lentil mixture in a blender or food processor. Remove center piece of blender lid (to allow steam to escape); secure blender lid on blender. Place a clean towel over opening in blender lid (to avoid splatters). Blend until smooth. Return pureed mixture to pan; stir in pepper.

4. Combine chopped dill and crème fraîche in a small bowl. Serve crème fraîche mixture on top of soup; garnish with dill sprigs, if desired. **Yield: 6 servings (serving size: about 1⅓ cups soup and 1 tablespoon crème fraîche mixture).**

CALORIES 187; FAT 6.1g (sat 3.3g, mono 1.4g, poly 0.4g); PROTEIN 8.5g; CARB 25.4g; FIBER 7.3g; CHOL 14mg; IRON 2.2mg; SODIUM 523mg; CALC 96mg

{vegan recipe}

Peanut and Squash Soup

1½   teaspoons peanut oil
 4   cups (½-inch) cubed peeled butternut squash
 1   cup chopped onion
 2   tablespoons minced garlic (about 6 cloves)
 ½   teaspoon salt
 ½   teaspoon ground cumin
 ¼   teaspoon ground coriander
 4   cups organic vegetable broth
 ¾   cup creamy peanut butter
 2   tablespoons tomato paste
 ½   teaspoon crushed red pepper
 ¼   cup chopped fresh cilantro

1. Heat peanut oil in a large saucepan over medium-high heat. Add squash and next 5 ingredients to pan; sauté 5 minutes or until onion is tender. Add broth and next 3 ingredients, stirring well to combine; bring to a boil. Reduce heat, and simmer 10 minutes or until squash is tender. Sprinkle with cilantro. **Yield: 6 servings (serving size: about 1 cup).**

CALORIES 303; FAT 17.8g (sat 3.6g, mono 8.4g, poly 4.9g); PROTEIN 10.4g; CARB 31.5g; FIBER 6g; CHOL 0mg; IRON 2.1mg; SODIUM 775mg; CALC 104mg

Winter Minestrone

If you prep all of the vegetables a day ahead, this soup will come together quickly just before your guests arrive.

- 2 teaspoons olive oil
- ½ cup chopped onion
- ½ teaspoon dried basil
- ½ teaspoon dried oregano
- 2 garlic cloves, minced
- 1¼ cups cubed peeled acorn or butternut squash (about 1 medium)
- ¾ cup diced zucchini
- ½ cup chopped carrot
- ½ cup diced fennel
- 1 cup water
- 1 (14-ounce) can organic vegetable broth
- 5 tablespoons no-salt-added tomato paste
- ¼ cup uncooked ditalini (very short tube-shaped pasta)
- 2½ cups chopped Swiss chard
- ½ cup rinsed and drained canned Great Northern beans
- ½ teaspoon freshly ground black pepper
- 2 tablespoons grated Asiago cheese

1. Heat oil in a Dutch oven over medium-high heat. Add onion and next 3 ingredients to pan; sauté 5 minutes or until onion is tender. Add squash and next 3 ingredients; sauté 5 minutes. Stir in 1 cup water, broth, and tomato paste; bring to a boil. Reduce heat, and simmer 10 minutes or until vegetables are crisp-tender. Stir in pasta; cook 8 minutes, stirring occasionally. Add chard; cook 3 minutes. Add beans; cook 2 minutes or until thoroughly heated. Stir in pepper. Serve with cheese.
Yield: 6 servings (serving size: about 1 cup minestrone and 1 teaspoon cheese).

CALORIES 102; FAT 2.5g (sat 0.7g, mono 1.4g, poly 0.2g); PROTEIN 4.5g; CARB 16.7g; FIBER 3.6g; CHOL 2mg; IRON 1.6mg; SODIUM 263mg; CALC 71mg

Black Bean Soup

1 pound dried black beans
4 cups organic vegetable broth
2 cups chopped onion
1 cup water
1 tablespoon ground cumin
3 bay leaves
1 serrano chile, finely chopped
2 tablespoons fresh lime juice
1 teaspoon kosher salt
¼ cup chopped fresh cilantro
3 tablespoons reduced-fat sour cream
Cilantro sprigs (optional)

1. Sort and wash beans; place in a large bowl. Cover with water to 2 inches above beans; cover and let stand 8 hours. Drain.

2. Combine beans, broth, and next 5 ingredients in an electric slow cooker. Cover and cook on LOW 10 hours. Discard bay leaves. Stir in juice and salt. Ladle 1½ cups soup into each of 6 bowls; sprinkle each with 2 teaspoons chopped cilantro. Top each serving with 1½ teaspoons sour cream. Garnish with cilantro sprigs, if desired. **Yield: 6 servings.**

CALORIES 288; FAT 2.3g (sat 0.9g, mono 0.4g, poly 0.5g); PROTEIN 18.5g; CARB 50g; FIBER 17.5g; CHOL 3mg; IRON 4.6mg; SODIUM 581mg; CALC 87mg

Serrano Chile
What it adds: This small, fiery chile is prized for its "back heat," which registers at the back of the throat. For less heat, seed the chile first or use a milder pepper, such as jalapeño. You can omit the chile altogether, if you prefer.

Sour Cream
What it adds: A dollop of sour cream provides a refreshing foil for this soup's spicy flavors.

Black Beans
What they add: Black beans are obviously the core of this soup, which is most certainly a good thing. They provide the majority of its protein (16 grams per serving), fiber (15.6 grams), and iron (3.8 milligrams).

kitchen how-to: make corn dumplings

Prepare the dumpling dough while the soup simmers.

1. Combine the masa harina and salt in a bowl. Add 3 tablespoons of hot water and 1 teaspoon of oil.

2. Stir the mixture with a fork until a soft dough forms. The dough will be dry.

3. Divide the dough into 24 pieces, shaping each into a ball.

4. Add the dumplings to the soup.

5. Cook, uncovered, 3 minutes or until the dumplings float.

kitchen how-to: make healthy creamy soups

When making soup, throwing in cream and butter isn't the only route to creamy success. You can create a rich, silky soup that isn't loaded with saturated fat by adding a punch of fresh flavor and color with herbs. Garnish the soup by scattering small, whole leaves or torn larger ones like basil, cilantro, or sage for a homey, rustic effect, or simply sprinkle on a variety of chopped fresh herbs. You can also finish the soup with a flavorful drizzle of pesto.

1. Sauté the aromatic ingredients in oil. This step coaxes the most flavor from pungent onions and garlic and also provides the building blocks for the soup.

2. Add your star vegetables— starches like potatoes or dried beans are popular, but almost any vegetables work. Finally, add stock, broth, or other liquid, season, and simmer the soup until the vegetables are tender.

3. The hallmark of a creamy soup is the smooth texture, so once the vegetables are cooked, puree them. Blenders, food processors, food mills, or immersion blenders can all do the trick, but the ingredients determine the tool; refer to the recipe for guidance.

Creamy Celeriac Soup

2 tablespoons butter
4 ounces French bread baguette, cut into
    1-inch cubes
1 tablespoon olive oil
3 cups sliced leek
2 tablespoons all-purpose flour
5 cups (1-inch) cubed peeled celeriac (celery root)
4 cups organic vegetable broth
½ cup half-and-half
½ teaspoon black pepper
¼ teaspoon salt
  Fresh parsley (optional)

1. Preheat oven to 350°.
2. Melt butter; toss with bread on a baking sheet.
Bake at 350° for 20 minutes or until golden.

3. Heat oil in a Dutch oven over medium heat. Add
leek; cook 10 minutes, stirring often. Stir in flour; cook
2 minutes, stirring well. Add celeriac and broth; bring to
a simmer. Cook for 30 minutes. Let stand 10 minutes.
4. Place half of mixture in blender. Remove center piece
of blender lid, and secure blender lid on blender. Place
a clean towel over opening in lid. Process until smooth.
Strain pureed mixture through a sieve over a bowl;
discard solids. Repeat procedure with remaining
celeriac mixture.
5. Return soup to pan over medium heat; stir in half-and-
half, pepper, and salt. Cook for 5 minutes. Serve with croutons. Garnish with parsley, if desired. **Yield: 4 servings
(serving size: 1½ cups soup and ½ cup croutons).**

CALORIES 356; FAT 14.1g (sat 6.6g, mono 4.3g, poly 1.3g); PROTEIN 11.1g; CARB 48.8g;
FIBER 6.5g; CHOL 26mg; IRON 4.5mg; SODIUM 906mg; CALC 185mg

kitchen how-to: peel celeriac (celery root)

Celeriac sounds like celery and has a related
flavor, but it couldn't look more different. It could easily
be mistaken for a dirty baseball, but once you peel away
its rough brown skin, you'll find a white, crisp flesh that
tastes like condensed celery.

1. Cut off the top and bottom of the celeriac, squaring
off the bottom so it will sit securely on the cutting
board.
2. Using a sharp knife, cut around the sides to remove
the outer layer. Then cut it according to your needs.

Creamy Cucumber Gazpacho

This easy soup comes together in less than 10 minutes.

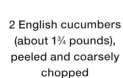 +  +

2 English cucumbers (about 1¾ pounds), peeled and coarsely chopped

2 cups organic vegetable broth

3 tablespoons white wine vinegar

 +

1 garlic clove, minced

3 cups fat-free sour cream

Place cucumbers, broth, vinegar, garlic, ¼ teaspoon salt, and ¼ teaspoon freshly ground black pepper in a blender; process until smooth. Pour cucumber mixture into a large bowl; add sour cream, stirring with a whisk until smooth. Cover and chill at least 2 hours. Ladle soup into bowls; top with finely chopped cucumber, if desired. **Yield: 8 servings (serving size: 1 cup).**

CALORIES 76; FAT 0g (sat 0g, mono 0g, poly 0g); PROTEIN 4.3g; CARB 15.4g; FIBER 0.9g; CHOL 8mg; IRON 0mg; SODIUM 336mg; CALC 107mg

{vegan recipe}
Carrot-Parsnip Soup with Parsnip Chips

Winter root vegetables lend their complementary, slightly sweet flavors to each bowlful of this hearty soup. Stir in more water or broth if you prefer a thinner consistency.

　2　tablespoons olive oil, divided
2½　cups chopped yellow onion
　3　cups coarsely chopped parsnip (about 1 pound)
　3　cups water
2½　cups coarsely chopped carrot (about 1 pound)
　2　(14-ounce) cans organic vegetable broth
¼　teaspoon salt
¼　teaspoon freshly ground black pepper
½　cup (⅛-inch-thick) slices parsnip
　1　tablespoon chopped fresh chives

1. Heat 1 teaspoon oil in a Dutch oven over medium heat. Add onion, and cook 10 minutes or until tender, stirring occasionally. Add chopped parsnip, water, carrot, and broth; bring to a boil. Reduce heat, and simmer 50 minutes or until vegetables are tender. Remove from heat; let stand 5 minutes.
2. Place half of carrot mixture in a blender; process until smooth. Pour pureed carrot mixture in a large bowl. Repeat procedure with remaining carrot mixture. Stir in salt and pepper.
3. Heat remaining 5 teaspoons oil in a small saucepan over medium-high heat. Add parsnip slices; cook 5 minutes or until lightly browned, turning occasionally. Drain on paper towels. Sprinkle parsnip chips and chives over soup.
Yield: 6 servings (serving size: 1⅓ cups soup, about 2 teaspoons parsnip chips, and ½ teaspoon chives).

CALORIES 159; FAT 4.9g (sat 0.7g, mono 3.4g, poly 0.6g); PROTEIN 3.7g; CARB 26.4g; FIBER 6.4g; CHOL 0mg; IRON 0.8mg; SODIUM 388mg; CALC 61mg

kitchen how-to: make parsnip chips

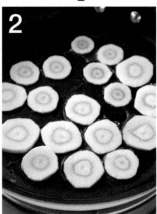

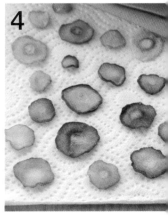

Parsnips are root vegetables with a sweet, nutty flavor. This long, tapering vegetable is shaped like a carrot but has beige-white skin.

1. Cut the parsnips into ⅛-inch-thick slices.

2. Heat oil in a small saucepan over medium-high heat. Add the parsnip slices.
3. Cook the parsnip slices 5 minutes or until lightly browned, turning them occasionally.
4. Drain the slices on paper towels.

Roasted Butternut Soup with Goat Cheese Toasts

Most any winter squash will work in this recipe. We like butternut for the nutty, slightly sweet flavor it lends to the soup. For a more filling entrée, pair this soup with a hearty salad studded with nuts and seeds.

  1 (2½-pound) butternut squash
     Cooking spray
  1 tablespoon extra-virgin olive oil
1½ cups chopped onion
  3 garlic cloves, minced
  6 cups Roasted Vegetable Stock
  2 cups coarsely chopped peeled Yukon gold potatoes
  2 teaspoons chopped fresh sage
  ¾ teaspoon salt
  ¼ teaspoon freshly ground black pepper
  1 bay leaf
  6 (1-ounce) slices French bread baguette
  ½ cup (2 ounces) goat cheese, crumbled
  1 tablespoon finely chopped fresh chives
  2 tablespoons chopped fresh parsley
  2 teaspoons honey

1. Preheat oven to 400°.
2. Cut squash in half lengthwise; discard seeds. Place squash, cut sides down, on a foil-lined baking sheet coated with cooking spray. Bake at 400° for 30 minutes or until tender. Cool. Discard peel; mash pulp.
3. Preheat broiler.
4. Heat a Dutch oven over medium-high heat. Add oil to pan; swirl to coat. Add onion; sauté 4 minutes, stirring occasionally. Add garlic; sauté 30 seconds, stirring constantly. Add squash, Roasted Vegetable Stock, and next 5 ingredients; bring to a boil. Reduce heat, and simmer 45 minutes or until potato is tender, stirring occasionally. Let stand 10 minutes. Discard bay leaf.
5. Place bread slices in a single layer on a baking sheet. Broil 2 minutes or until toasted. Sprinkle about 4 teaspoons cheese on each slice; sprinkle evenly with chives.
6. Place one-third of vegetable mixture in a blender. Remove center piece of blender lid (to allow steam to escape); secure blender lid on blender. Place a clean towel over opening in blender lid (to avoid splatters). Blend until smooth. Pour into a large bowl. Repeat procedure twice with remaining squash mixture. Return pureed mixture to pan; cook over medium heat 3 minutes or until thoroughly heated. Stir in parsley and honey. Serve with toasts. **Yield: 6 servings (serving size: about 1 cup soup and 1 toast).**

CALORIES 292; FAT 10.1g (sat 3g, mono 5.7g, poly 1.2g); PROTEIN 7.3g; CARB 47.8g; FIBER 5g; CHOL 7mg; IRON 2.6mg; SODIUM 546mg; CALC 126mg

{vegan recipe}
Roasted Vegetable Stock

1 whole garlic head
2 cups (1-inch) sliced onion
1½ cups (1-inch) sliced carrot
1 cup (1-inch) sliced celery
2 medium turnips, peeled and each cut into 3 wedges
½ teaspoon black pepper
2 tablespoons extra-virgin olive oil
2 cups (1-inch) slices leek
8 ounces whole cremini mushrooms
½ cup dry white wine
10 cups water

4 fresh parsley sprigs
4 fresh thyme sprigs
1 bay leaf

1. Preheat oven to 450°.
2. Cut off pointed end of garlic just to expose cloves. Place garlic and next 4 ingredients on a large jelly-roll pan. Sprinkle with pepper, and drizzle with oil; toss well. Bake at 450° for 10 minutes. Add leek and mushrooms. Bake an additional 35 minutes or until browned and tender, stirring occasionally. Spoon vegetables into a

Dutch oven. Pour wine into jelly-roll pan, scraping to loosen browned bits. Add wine mixture, 10 cups water, and remaining ingredients to vegetable mixture; bring to a boil. Reduce heat, and simmer 1 hour, stirring occasionally. Strain through a fine sieve over a bowl; discard solids. Store in an airtight container in the refrigerator for up to 1 week. **Yield: 7 cups (serving size: 1 cup).**

CALORIES 50; FAT 4.7g (sat 0.7g, mono 3.3g, poly 0.7g); PROTEIN 0.4g; CARB 2.2g; FIBER 0.4g; CHOL 0mg; IRON 0.2mg; SODIUM 8mg; CALC 9mg

kitchen how-to: make goat cheese toasts

1

2

3

These toasts provide a crunchy, tangy contrast to creamy soups.

4

1. Cut a baguette into 1-ounce slices. Place bread slices in a single layer on a baking sheet.
2. Broil the slices 2 minutes or until toasted.
3. Sprinkle about 4 teaspoons of crumbled goat cheese on each slice.
4. Sprinkle evenly with chives.

stews

With less liquid and a chunkier texture than soups, these slow-simmered one-pot dishes are comforting and filling.

African Ground Nut Stew with Sour Cream-Chive Topping

Peanuts, which are a staple in African cuisine, are also called ground nuts to distinguish them from tree nuts. For more intense heat, use a full teaspoon of crushed red pepper. Garnish this stew with chives, if desired.

  1   cup fat-free sour cream
  ¼   cup minced fresh chives
  2   teaspoons canola oil
  1¼ cups thinly sliced yellow onion
  ¾   cup chopped red bell pepper
  3   garlic cloves, minced
  1   cup chopped unsalted, dry-roasted
       peanuts
  1   teaspoon salt
  ½   to 1 teaspoon crushed red pepper
  4   cups (1-inch) cubed peeled sweet potatoes
       (about 1½ pounds)
  2½ cups quartered small red potatoes (about
       1 pound)
  2½ cups organic vegetable broth (such as
       Swanson Certified Organic)
  1   (28-ounce) can diced tomatoes, undrained

1. Combine sour cream and chives in a small bowl; cover. Refrigerate 2 hours.
2. Heat oil in a Dutch oven over medium-high heat. Add onion and bell pepper; sauté 3 minutes or until tender. Add garlic; sauté 30 seconds. Stir in peanuts, salt, and crushed red pepper; sauté 2 minutes. Add potatoes, broth, and tomatoes; bring to a boil. Cover, reduce heat, and simmer 1 hour and 10 minutes or until the potatoes are tender. Place 1⅔ cups stew into each of 6 bowls; top each serving with about 2½ tablespoons sour cream mixture. **Yield: 6 servings.**

CALORIES 416; FAT 14g (sat 1.9g, mono 6.9g, poly 4.5g); PROTEIN 14.1g; CARB 62g; FIBER 10g; CHOL 7mg; IRON 2.4mg; SODIUM 882mg; CALC 175mg

all about taming spicy heat

Fiery foods demand the balance of cool accompaniments to tame their heat, but sometimes the damage is already done. A word of warning: Be careful what you reach for after a spicy bite. Water spreads capsaicin—the heat-producing agent in chile peppers—and fizzy beverages only make things worse. One possible exception is beer because alcohol tends to conquer capsaicin. Here are some other ways to ease the burn when spicy heat has already hit you.

• Dairy products such as milk, cheese, sour cream, and yogurt coat the mouth and throat with casein, a protein that counters the alkaloids that give chiles their heat.

• Chocolate is another source of casein and has long been used to balance spicy chiles in some versions of mole, the classic Mexican sauce.

• Some beans contain casein, and refried beans often accompany Mexican dishes.

• Citrus fruits can counteract spice from a chile, possibly by counteracting its alkalinity, rendering the heat-causing oils less effective. The cooling qualities of citrus fruits may explain the preference for margaritas and lemony iced tea with Tex-Mex fare.

• Sugar cools the burn, so sweet lemonade would be a good choice, although sweetened fruit juices of any kind will help.

{ vegan recipe }

Smoky Seitan, Pinto Bean, and Hominy Stew

For a fun presentation, serve this satisfying vegetarian stew in roasted, seeded acorn squash halves.

1	tablespoon canola oil
1½	cups diced white onion (about 1 large)
1	cup diced celery (about 2 stalks)
¾	cup diced carrot (about 1 large)
1	cup diced green bell pepper (about 1)
1	teaspoon minced garlic
2	cups organic vegetable broth (such as Swanson Certified Organic)
1	teaspoon chili powder
½	teaspoon salt
½	teaspoon chipotle chile powder
1	(28-ounce) can diced tomatoes, undrained
1	pound seitan, cubed
1	(15.5-ounce) can white hominy, rinsed and drained
1	(15-ounce) can pinto beans, rinsed and drained

1. Heat oil in a Dutch oven over medium-high heat. Add onion and next 4 ingredients to pan; sauté 5 minutes. Add broth and remaining ingredients to pan; bring to a boil. Reduce heat, and simmer 15 minutes or until vegetables are tender. **Yield: 8 servings (serving size: 1 cup).**

CALORIES 319; FAT 3.5g (sat 0.4g, mono 1.3g, poly 1.3g); PROTEIN 46g; CARB 27.2g; FIBER 5.2g; CHOL 0mg; IRON 4.1mg; SODIUM 488mg; CALC 128mg

Chipotle Chile Powder
What it adds: Chipotle chile powder lends wonderful smoky flavor to this hearty stew.

White Hominy
What it adds: A traditional Native American ingredient, hominy is nutty and tender. It's made from dried, hulled corn kernels; white hominy is made from white corn kernels.

Seitan
What it adds: Seitan (pronounced say-tahn), which is also known as wheat gluten, is made from the protein portion of wheat. It provides nearly a day's worth of protein in one serving of this dish.

kitchen how-to:
peel turnips

Because of their small size, it's best to use a fork rather than your hands to hold the turnip stable. Then use a vegetable peeler to remove the skin.

all about buying turnips

Fresh turnips are usually available year-round, but their peak season is October through February. Choose turnips that feel heavy for their size—these are the young ones, and they'll be more delicately flavored and textured than older ones. The roots should be firm, and the greens, if they're still attached, should look fresh and bright.

{vegan recipe}
Chickpea and Winter Vegetable Stew

2 teaspoons extra-virgin olive oil
1 cup chopped onion
1 cup (½-inch) sliced leek
½ teaspoon ground coriander
½ teaspoon caraway seeds, crushed
⅛ teaspoon ground cumin
⅛ teaspoon ground red pepper
1 garlic clove, minced
3⅔ cups Simple Vegetable Stock, divided
2 cups (1-inch) cubed peeled butternut squash
1 cup (½-inch) sliced carrot
¾ cup (1-inch) cubed peeled Yukon gold potato
1 tablespoon harissa
1½ teaspoons tomato paste
¾ teaspoon salt
1 pound turnips, peeled and each cut into 8 wedges (about 2 medium)
1 (15½-ounce) can chickpeas (garbanzo beans), drained
¼ cup chopped fresh flat-leaf parsley
1½ teaspoons honey
1⅓ cups uncooked couscous
8 lemon wedges

1. Heat oil in a large saucepan over medium-high heat. Add onion and leek; sauté 5 minutes. Add coriander and next 4 ingredients; cook 1 minute, stirring constantly. Add 3 cups Simple Vegetable Stock and the next 8 ingredients; bring to a boil. Cover, reduce heat, and simmer 30 minutes. Stir in parsley and honey.
2. Remove ⅔ cup hot cooking liquid from squash mixture. Place cooking liquid and remaining ⅔ cup stock in a medium bowl. Stir in couscous. Cover and let stand 5 minutes. Fluff with a fork. Serve with lemon wedges.
Yield: 8 servings (serving size: ¾ cup squash mixture, ½ cup couscous, and 1 lemon wedge).

CALORIES 264; FAT 2.3g (sat 0.3g,mono 1g,poly 0.6g); PROTEIN 8.3g; CARB 54.5g; FIBER 7.5g; CHOL 0mg; IRON 2.4mg; SODIUM 425mg; CALC 92mg

{ vegan recipe }
Simple Vegetable Stock

1 whole garlic head
10 cups water
2 cups (1-inch) sliced onion
2 cups (1-inch) sliced leek
1 cup (1-inch) sliced carrot
1 cup (1-inch) sliced celery
1 small turnip (about ¼ pound), peeled and cut into 8 wedges
¼ pound cremini mushrooms, halved
6 black peppercorns
4 parsley sprigs
4 thyme sprigs
1 bay leaf

1. Cut off pointed end of garlic just to expose cloves.
2. Combine garlic and remaining ingredients in a Dutch oven; bring to a boil. Reduce heat, and simmer 50 minutes. Strain through a fine sieve over a bowl; discard solids. Store in an airtight container in the refrigerator for up to 1 week. **Yield: 7 cups (serving size: 1 cup).**

CALORIES 6; FAT 0g (sat 0g, mono 0g, poly 0g); PROTEIN 0.2g; CARB 1.3g; FIBER 0.3g; CHOL 0mg; IRON 0.1mg; SODIUM 4mg; CALC 5mg

{ vegan recipe }

Lentil-Edamame Stew

Fava beans are traditional in this stew, which we updated with edamame. You can also substitute green peas for the edamame, if you like. Scoop up this thick stew with pita. Halve the portion if you'd like to serve it as a hearty side dish.

1 **cup dried lentils**
¾ **cup frozen shelled edamame (green soybeans)**
2 **tablespoons olive oil**
1½ **cups minced red onion**
3 **garlic cloves, minced**
1 **(14.5-ounce) can diced tomatoes, undrained**
6 **tablespoons fresh lemon juice**
1 **tablespoon chopped fresh parsley**
1 **tablespoon chopped fresh mint**
½ **teaspoon salt**
½ **teaspoon ground cumin**
⅛ **teaspoon ground red pepper**
⅛ **teaspoon ground cinnamon**
Dash of ground cloves

1. Place lentils in a large saucepan; cover with water to 2 inches above lentils. Bring to a boil; cover, reduce heat, and simmer 20 minutes or until tender. Drain well, and set aside.
2. Place edamame in a small saucepan; cover with water to 2 inches above edamame. Bring to a boil; cook 2 minutes or until edamame are tender. Remove from heat; drain well.
3. Heat oil in a Dutch oven over medium-high heat. Add onion, garlic, and tomatoes to pan; sauté 6 minutes or until onion is translucent, stirring often. Stir in lentils, edamame, lemon juice, and remaining ingredients. Cook 2 minutes or until thoroughly heated, stirring often. **Yield: 4 servings (serving size: about 1 cup).**

CALORIES 320; FAT 8g (sat 1.1g, mono 5.2g, poly 1.4g); PROTEIN 18.6g; CARB 48.4g; FIBER 10.7g; CHOL 0mg; IRON 5.7mg; SODIUM 432mg; CALC 59mg

all about edamame

Edamame, the Japanese word for fresh soybeans, have a sweet, nutty flavor and velvety texture. These tasty beans provides 14.5 grams of protein in a half cup. They also pack vitamin A, fiber, calcium, and antioxidants.

{ vegan recipe }

Three-Bean Vegetarian Chili

Cumin and paprika add earthy flavor to this chili. Serve with a hearty salad and corn bread.

    2   red bell peppers
    3   tablespoons extra-virgin olive oil
    1   cup chopped onion
    2   teaspoons ground cumin
    1   teaspoon crushed red pepper
    1   teaspoon paprika
    ½   teaspoon salt
    4   garlic cloves, thinly sliced
    2   cups organic vegetable broth
    1½ cups (½-inch) cubed peeled butternut squash
    1   (28-ounce) can no-salt-added tomatoes, undrained and chopped
    1   (15-ounce) can pinto beans, rinsed and drained
    1   (15-ounce) can cannellini beans, rinsed and drained
    1   (15-ounce) can red kidney beans, rinsed and drained
    ½   cup thinly sliced green onions

1. Preheat broiler.
2. Cut bell peppers in half lengthwise; remove and discard seeds and membranes. Place pepper halves, skin sides up, on a foil-lined baking sheet. Broil 15 minutes or until blackened. Place pepper halves in a zip-top plastic bag; seal. Let stand 15 minutes. Peel and chop peppers.
3. Heat a Dutch oven over medium-low heat. Add oil to pan; swirl to coat. Add onion; cook 15 minutes, stirring occasionally. Stir in cumin and next 4 ingredients; cook 2 minutes, stirring frequently. Add bell peppers, broth, squash, and tomatoes; bring to a simmer. Cook 20 minutes, stirring occasionally. Add beans; simmer 25 minutes or until slightly thick, stirring occasionally. Sprinkle with green onions. **Yield: 6 servings (serving size: about 1½ cups).**

CALORIES 264; FAT 8.3g (sat 1.2g, mono 5.2g, poly 1.3g); PROTEIN 9.5g; CARB 40.9g; FIBER 10.7g; CHOL 0mg; IRON 4.4mg; SODIUM 787mg; CALC 145mg

kitchen how-to: make vegetarian chili

Vegetarian chilis rely on tomatoes and beans as their base, but there are ways to take a traditional chili recipe to the next level. One is to roast bell peppers or, for a fiery hit, broil chile peppers to add smoky flavor (see pages 24 and 205 for information about roasting and broiling peppers). There are hundreds of different chile options, and each contributes a slightly different flavor—from fruity to bitter with varying heat levels. For example, poblanos offer mild heat and a fruity taste. Jalapeños have a sharp, acidic flavor and a medium heat level—if you want to tame that heat, remove the seeds and membranes on the inside walls. Or use serrano peppers to crank up the heat even more. Fresh peppers are best in quick-cooking chili, but for those that simmer more than two hours, try dried peppers, or use a combination for more nuanced flavor.

1. The first step is to cook aromatic ingredients such as onions and garlic in a small amount of oil to add depth to the chili. Cook them for about 15 minutes or until they're browned.

2. Add any spices and flavorings you wish (cumin, crushed red pepper, and salt are favorites), and then add the vegetables, such as squash and tomatoes, and broth for color. Bring the mixture to a simmer, and cook for 20 minutes, stirring occasionally.

3. Add a variety of beans to the simmering pot. This will provide color and texture and also amp up the protein. Canned beans are convenient options, but you can also prepare dried beans (see page 171) to help lower the sodium content, if you'd like. You'll need to simmer the chili for 25 minutes or until the mixture becomes slightly thick, stirring occasionally. Sprinkle the chili with any garnish you'd like, such as fresh herbs or chopped green onions, before serving it.

Ingredient Substitution Guide

If you're right in the middle of cooking and realize you don't have
a particular ingredient, refer to the substitutions in this list.

Ingredient	Substitution
Baking Products	
Baking powder, 1 teaspoon	½ teaspoon cream of tartar and ¼ teaspoon baking soda
Chocolate	
Semisweet, 1 ounce	1 ounce unsweetened chocolate and 1 tablespoon sugar
Unsweetened, 1 ounce	3 tablespoons cocoa and 1 tablespoon butter or margarine
Cocoa, ¼ cup	1 ounce unsweetened chocolate (decrease fat in recipe by ½ tablespoon)
Coconut, fresh, grated, 1½ tablespoons	1 tablespoon flaked coconut
Cornstarch, 1 tablespoon	2 tablespoons all-purpose flour or granular tapioca
Flour	
All-purpose, 1 tablespoon	1½ teaspoons cornstarch, potato starch, or rice starch
Cake, 1 cup sifted	1 cup minus 2 tablespoons all-purpose flour
Self-rising, 1 cup	1 cup all-purpose flour, 1 teaspoon baking powder, and ½ teaspoon salt
Sugar, Powdered, 1 cup	1 cup sugar and 1 tablespoon cornstarch (processed in food processor)
Honey, ½ cup	½ cup molasses or maple syrup
Eggs	
1 large	2 egg yolks for custards and cream fillings or 2 egg yolks and 1 tablespoon water for cookies
1 large	¼ cup egg substitute
2 large	3 small eggs
1 egg white (2 tablespoons)	2 tablespoons egg substitute
1 egg yolk (1½ tablespoons)	2 tablespoons sifted dry egg yolk powder and 2 teaspoons water or 1½ tablespoons thawed frozen egg yolk
Fruits and Vegetables	
Lemon, 1 medium	2 to 3 tablespoons juice and 2 teaspoons grated rind
Juice, 1 teaspoon	½ teaspoon vinegar
Peel, dried	2 teaspoons freshly grated lemon rind
Orange, 1 medium	½ cup juice and 2 tablespoons grated rind
Tomatoes, fresh, chopped, 2 cups	1 (16-ounce) can (may need to drain)
Tomato juice, 1 cup	½ cup tomato sauce and ½ cup water
Tomato sauce, 2 cups	¾ cup tomato paste and 1 cup water

Ingredient	Substitution
Dairy Products	
Milk	
Buttermilk, low-fat or fat-free, 1 cup	1 tablespoon lemon juice or vinegar and 1 cup low-fat or fat-free milk (let stand 10 minutes)
Fat-free milk, 1 cup	4 to 5 tablespoons fat-free dry milk powder; enough cold water to make 1 cup
Sour cream, 1 cup	1 cup plain yogurt
Miscellaneous	
Broth, beef or chicken, canned, 1 cup	1 bouillon cube dissolved in 1 cup boiling water
Capers, 1 tablespoon	1 tablespoon chopped dill pickles or green olives
Chile paste, 1 teaspoon	¼ teaspoon hot red pepper flakes
Chili sauce, 1 cup	1 cup tomato sauce, ¼ cup brown sugar, 2 tablespoons vinegar, ¼ teaspoon ground cinnamon, dash of ground cloves, and dash of ground allspice
Ketchup, 1 cup	1 cup tomato sauce, ½ cup sugar, and 2 tablespoons vinegar (for cooking; not to be used as a condiment)
Tahini (sesame-seed paste), 1 cup	¾ cup creamy peanut butter and ¼ cup sesame oil
Vinegar, cider, 1 teaspoon	2 teaspoons lemon juice mixed with a pinch of sugar
Wasabi, 1 teaspoon	1 teaspoon horseradish or hot dry mustard
Seasonings	
Allspice, ground, 1 teaspoon	½ teaspoon ground cinnamon and ½ teaspoon ground cloves
Apple pie spice, 1 teaspoon	½ teaspoon ground cinnamon, ¼ teaspoon ground nutmeg, and ⅛ teaspoon ground cardamom
Bay leaf, 1 whole	¼ teaspoon crushed bay leaf
Chives, chopped, 1 tablespoon	1 tablespoon chopped green onion tops
Garlic, 1 clove	1 teaspoon bottled minced garlic
Ginger	
Crystallized, 1 tablespoon	⅛ teaspoon ground ginger
Fresh, grated, 1 tablespoon	⅛ teaspoon ground ginger
Herbs, fresh, 1 tablespoon	1 teaspoon dried herbs or ¼ teaspoon ground herbs (except rosemary)
Horseradish, fresh, grated, 1 tablespoon	2 tablespoons prepared horseradish
Lemongrass, 1 stalk, chopped	1 teaspoon grated lemon zest
Mint, fresh, chopped, 3 tablespoons	1 tablespoon dried spearmint or peppermint
Mustard, dried, 1 teaspoon	1 tablespoon prepared mustard
Parsley, fresh, chopped, 1 tablespoon	1 teaspoon dried parsley
Vanilla bean, 6-inch bean	1 tablespoon vanilla extract

Nutritional Analysis

How to Use It and Why

Glance at the end of any *Cooking Light* recipe, and you'll see how committed we are to helping you make the best of today's light cooking. With chefs, registered dietitians, home economists, and a computer system that analyzes every ingredient we use, *Cooking Light* gives you authoritative dietary detail like no other magazine. We go to such lengths so you can see how our recipes fit into your healthful eating plan. If you're trying to lose weight, the calorie and fat figures will probably help most. But if you're keeping a close eye on the sodium, cholesterol, and saturated fat in your diet, we provide those numbers, too. And because many women don't get enough iron or calcium, we can also help there, as well. Finally, there's a fiber analysis for those of us who don't get enough roughage.

Here's a helpful guide to put our nutritional analysis numbers into perspective. Remember, one size doesn't fit all, so take your lifestyle, age, and circumstances into consideration when determining your nutrition needs. For example, pregnant or breast-feeding women need more protein, calories, and calcium. And women older than 50 need 1,200mg of calcium daily, 200mg more than the amount recommended for younger women and men.

We Use These Abbreviations in Our Nutritional Analysis

sat saturated fat
mono monounsaturated fat
poly polyunsaturated fat
CARB carbohydrates

CHOL cholesterol
CALC calcium
g gram
mg milligram

Daily Nutrition Guide

	Women Ages 25 to 50	Women over 50	Men over 24
Calories	2,000	2,000 or less	2,700
Protein	50g	50g or less	63g
Fat	65g or less	65g or less	88g or less
Saturated Fat	20g or less	20g or less	27g or less
Carbohydrates	304g	304g	410g
Fiber	25g to 35g	25g to 35g	25g to 35g
Cholesterol	300mg or less	300mg or less	300mg or less
Iron	18mg	8mg	8mg
Sodium	2,300mg or less	1,500mg or less	2,300mg or less
Calcium	1,000mg	1,200mg	1,000mg

The nutritional values used in our calculations either come from The Food Processor, Version 8.9 (ESHA Research), or are provided by food manufacturers.

Seasonal Produce Guide

When you use fresh fruits, vegetables, and herbs, you don't have to do much to make them taste great. Although many fruits, vegetables, and herbs are available year-round, you'll get better flavor and prices when you buy what's in season. The Seasonal Produce Guide below helps you choose the best produce so you can create sensational meals all year long.

Spring

Fruits
Bananas
Blood oranges
Coconuts
Grapefruit
Kiwifruit
Lemons
Limes
Mangoes
Navel oranges
Papayas
Passionfruit
Pineapples
Strawberries
Tangerines
Valencia oranges

Vegetables
Artichokes
Arugula
Asparagus
Avocados
Baby leeks
Beets
Belgian endive
Broccoli
Cauliflower
Dandelion
  greens
Fava beans
Green onions
Green peas
Kale
Lettuce
Mushrooms
Radishes
Red potatoes
Rhubarb
Snap beans
Snow peas
Spinach
Sugar snap peas
Sweet onions
Swiss chard

Herbs
Chives
Dill
Garlic chives
Lemongrass
Mint
Parsley
Thyme

Summer

Fruits
Blackberries
Blueberries
Boysenberries
Cantaloupes
Casaba melons
Cherries
Crenshaw melons
Grapes
Guava
Honeydew melons
Mangoes
Nectarines
Papayas
Peaches
Plums
Raspberries
Strawberries
Watermelons

Vegetables
Avocados
Beets
Bell peppers
Cabbage
Carrots
Celery
Chili peppers
Collards
Corn
Cucumbers
Eggplant
Green beans
Jicama
Lima beans
Okra
Pattypan squash
Peas
Radicchio
Radishes
Summer squash
Tomatoes

Herbs
Basil
Bay leaves
Borage
Chives
Cilantro
Dill
Lavender
Lemon balm
Marjoram
Mint
Oregano
Rosemary
Sage
Summer savory
Tarragon
Thyme

Autumn

Fruits
Apples
Cranberries
Figs
Grapes
Pears
Persimmons
Pomegranates
Quinces

Vegetables
Belgian endive
Bell peppers
Broccoli
Brussels
  sprouts
Cabbage
Cauliflower
Eggplant
Escarole
Fennel
Frisée
Leeks
Mushrooms
Parsnips
Pumpkins
Red potatoes
Rutabagas
Shallots
Sweet potatoes
Winter squash
Yukon gold
  potatoes

Herbs
Basil
Bay leaves
Parsley
Rosemary
Sage
Tarragon
Thyme

Winter

Fruits
Apples
Blood oranges
Cranberries
Grapefruit
Kiwifruit
Kumquats
Lemons
Limes
Mandarin oranges
Navel oranges
Pears
Persimmons
Pomegranates
Pomelos
Tangelos
Tangerines
Quinces

Vegetables
Baby turnips
Beets
Belgian endive
Brussels sprouts
Celery root
Chili peppers
Dried beans
Escarole
Fennel
Frisée
Jerusalem
  artichokes
Kale
Leeks
Mushrooms
Parsnips
Potatoes
Rutabagas
Sweet potatoes
Turnips
Watercress
Winter squash

Herbs
Bay leaves
Chives
Parsley
Rosemary
Sage
Thyme

Metric Equivalents

The information in the following charts is provided to help cooks outside the United States successfully use the recipes in this book. All equivalents are approximate.

Cooking/Oven Temperatures

	Fahrenheit	Celsius	Gas Mark
Freeze Water	32° F	0° C	
Room Temp.	68° F	20° C	
Boil Water	212° F	100° C	
Bake	325° F	160° C	3
	350° F	180° C	4
	375° F	190° C	5
	400° F	200° C	6
	425° F	220° C	7
	450° F	230° C	8
Broil			Grill

Liquid Ingredients by Volume

¼ tsp	=	1 ml						
½ tsp	=	2 ml						
1 tsp	=	5 ml						
3 tsp	=	1 tbl	=	½ fl oz	=	15 ml		
2 tbls	=	⅛ cup	=	1 fl oz	=	30 ml		
4 tbls	=	¼ cup	=	2 fl oz	=	60 ml		
5⅓ tbls	=	⅓ cup	=	3 fl oz	=	80 ml		
8 tbls	=	½ cup	=	4 fl oz	=	120 ml		
10⅔ tbls	=	⅔ cup	=	5 fl oz	=	160 ml		
12 tbls	=	¾ cup	=	6 fl oz	=	180 ml		
16 tbls	=	1 cup	=	8 fl oz	=	240 ml		
1 pt	=	2 cups	=	16 fl oz	=	480 ml		
1 qt	=	4 cups	=	32 fl oz	=	960 ml		
				33 fl oz	=	1000 ml	=	1 l

Dry Ingredients by Weight

(To convert ounces to grams, multiply the number of ounces by 30.)

1 oz	=	⅟₁₆ lb	=	30 g
4 oz	=	¼ lb	=	120 g
8 oz	=	½ lb	=	240 g
12 oz	=	¾ lb	=	360 g
16 oz	=	1 lb	=	480 g

Length

(To convert inches to centimeters, multiply the number of inches by 2.5.)

1 in	=				2.5 cm		
6 in	=	½ ft		=	15 cm		
12 in	=	1 ft		=	30 cm		
36 in	=	3 ft	=	1 yd	=	90 cm	
40 in	=				100 cm	=	1 m

Equivalents for Different Types of Ingredients

Standard Cup	Fine Powder (ex. flour)	Grain (ex. rice)	Granular (ex. sugar)	Liquid Solids (ex. butter)	Liquid (ex. milk)
1	140 g	150 g	190 g	200 g	240 ml
¾	105 g	113 g	143 g	150 g	180 ml
⅔	93 g	100 g	125 g	133 g	160 ml
½	70 g	75 g	95 g	100 g	120 ml
⅓	47 g	50 g	63 g	67 g	80 ml
¼	35 g	38 g	48 g	50 g	60 ml
⅛	18 g	19 g	24 g	25 g	30 ml

subject index

recipe title index